C. J. Anderson-Wu

Endangered Youth

Taiwan, Hong Kong, Ukraine

A Collection of Short/Micro Fiction

Preface—Cry Freedom

When I started writing about White Terror in Taiwan, thirty years had passed since the abolishment of Martial Law (1949-1987), and political censorship had been completely lifted in Taiwan. Today, writing anything political in Taiwan is safe, no matter how controversial it is. There are no longer secret arrests, unwarranted raids at one's home or office, executions or incarcerations without open trial, intrusive surveillance openly targeting those people under watch, or harassment from law enforcement on dissidents and their families, their acquaintances, and even their employers and co-workers.

Reestablishing the Lost History

With more and more information regarding the highly oppressive political climate during the rule of Martial Law, Taiwanese people are stunned to know that, all what we had been taught and told, and all what we had believed to be true, were lies. Thus recovering a more authentic recent history of Taiwan with multiple facets became a gigantic construction of the society as a whole. But how and where to start? When the sealed archives are open, we question whether they were more unfound or had been destroyed. When victims are interviewed, we wonder if their memories are reliable. When cases are reinvestigated, we ask, where are the identities of the perpetrators?

More questions are raised. Why weren't the perpetrators punished? Would those political dissidents who paid tremendous prices for their activism choose the same path if they were given the chance to make decisions again? Were they really, according to the unearthed materials, planning to overturn the government? Were they really members or sympathizers with the enemy, the Communist Party? Why was campaigning for Taiwan's independence, the de facto status of Taiwan since WWII, a taboo? Were they too naive to believe they could change the world? Were they really idealists and ready to sacrifice for their idealism? Or, were they the victims of indiscriminate persecution?

Moreover, when the late justice eventually could come, through the measures of "Transitional Justice", what are we trying to recover from it? What lessons can we learn from it? What would be the best way to compensate each of those who had been wronged? In addition to their lives, their freedom and their dignity, what else had been lost because of the injustice? None of these questions can be answered easily, and the multiple layers of challenges and dilemmas can be only contemplated upon through dramatized episodes without expecting oversimplified solutions.

Breaking away from propagandic writing and leaving behind the sadistic censorship during the rule of Martial Law, literary works thrive in Taiwan. Many of them are created based on the new discoveries of injustice and human rights violations in the past. Some of these works set out from personal memories, some look into unknown family histories, some attempt to draw out large pictures of what really could have happened during the shadowed years not very long ago. Thanks to the political reforms Taiwan eventually accomplished and the democracy we worked so hard to sustain, a variety of approaches have been experimented with and employed to deal with the unspeakable pain, regret, anger, grief and shame.

But we are far from a happy ending.

If We Did Not Correct It Sooner, Can You?

In 2014, when there were more than one million people participating in the Umbrella Movement in Hong Kong, people in Taiwan thought democracy would eventually prevail. In 2019, when there were close to two million people walking in the streets to protest the extradition bill in Hong Kong, we thought freedom certainly would win. There were never demonstrations of such scale in Taiwan during the Martial Law period; under very tight control and very terrifying law and order policies, it took Taiwan fifty years to establish a real democracy through sporadic resistance and actions.

We were so wrong about Hong Kong. Under the very severe National Security Law, the openness of a society could be destroyed overnight, freedom of speech could disappear in a blink of an eye. Unwarranted raids, secret arrests, incarceration without trial, or cruel sentences after extremely distorted court hearings that had faded into the history in Taiwan were now happening daily in Hong Kong. Many Hong Kongers choose to leave home, if they could afford living in another county, but activists who stay in Hong Kong are isolated. History repeats itself, like a rewinding film, and for people in Taiwan, it is very hard to watch it again. Beside providing shelter or some underground connections, what can the world do to support the civil rights movement in Hong Kong?

During the White Terror period, Taiwan's connection with the world had been shut down by its dictatorial ruler. Not until the Formosa Incident in 1979, did the world know about the horrifying fates of many dissidents and political prisoners. Without the pressure from the international society, many defendants of the Formosa Trial undoubtedly would have been sentenced to death or put into relentlessly long incarceration. But even in a digital era, Hong Kong people's cries for freedom were not fully heard by the world.

The turmoil in Hong Kong reminded Taiwanese people of the dark years of the White Terror. The past lessons taught us that silence certainly is not a solution. A bystander might remain silent at first when seeing injustice done to others, but the disaster eventually will befall on everyone when there is no intervention to stop the violence. Moreover, how can we expect others to fight for the values we believe in? Can we enjoy the achievement of democracy at the price of other people's lives, freedom, or dignity?

Then in February 2022, Ukraine was invaded by Russian troops. People in Hong Kong and Taiwan were tremendously vexed. In an open letter to Ukrainian people, an anonymous Hong Kong activist said:

"You may not realise what Ukraine means to us in Hong Kong. Since our Umbrella Revolution in 2014, many of us have been inspired by the Euromaidan in imagining a better democratic movement, particularly in the debate over non-violence versus a militant approach to the struggle…With police brutality, torture and deaths becoming routine, we came to understand the heavy price of fighting for freedom, and yet more and more of us decided to do so…

Putin uses ultranationalism and an imagined historical claim to justify invasion. We are all too familiar with such rhetoric. The Chinese Communist Party has been feeding us the same story for more than a decade, trying to convince us there are no alternatives besides relying on 'the motherland', while at the same time destroying our value system, local language and politics by every means, whether gradual or abrupt."

Compared to the shocking military offenses to Ukraine, offenses on Hong Kong people by armed forces, though relatively smaller in scale and with less bloodshed, are less known by the international society. What appalls us is, many people still don't think that the cruelty towards the Hong Kong people, the Tibetan people and the Uyghur People is real. And some people calling themselves liberals contend that Hong Kong's problems are Chinese domestic issues and should be left to the Chinese government, despite the serious human rights violations of the Chinese regime.

Political debates and historical narratives have failed to capture the personal plight of individuals—their hopes, fears, regrets, anger, and losses. Drawing inspiration from real incidents and characters, the stories in *Endangered Youth* endeavor to represent the complex dilemmas, pains, despairs, courage, and determination people have encountered in their pursuit of freedom and justice. Literature not only provides us artistic perspectives but also reveals the truths of human nature. History has taught us that redemption lies not in heroism, but in acknowledging our weaknesses, cowardice, and selfishness. Through insightful and personal perspectives conveyed in literary works, we come to understand both the glorious and dark aspects of ourselves, allowing us to anticipate opportunities to prevent the repetition of tragedies at the earliest possible moment.

Can we?

Contents

- 3   Preface—Cry Freedom
- 12   A Letter from the Son of A Dissident to the Son of A Dissident
- 18   June
- 30   Endangered Youth
- 42   Grandpa Fu's Suitcase
- 49   Grandpa Fu's Roommate
- 62   9066 Soup
- 77   Pronunciation Practice
- 89   Over the Other Side of the Road
- 91   A Collector of Indigenous Songs
- 93   A Bystander of His Hometown
- 96   Millions of Ants
- 107   It Took Us 50 Years
- 120   I Am Not Broken
- 130   In Your Eyes, I See
- 133   Political Prisoners
- 135   Prison Break
- 137   He and Darkness Become One

140	Glossary for the Trial of National Security Law in Hong Kong
143	Bookstore Owners in Hong Kong
145	Handbook of Conflict Avoidance
147	Freedom of Sp.e..e…c…What did you say?
152	Un(found) Poetry—A Fiction
155	Our Burials at Sea
157	Rest, Not In Peace
160	I Died Three Years Ago
163	I Am Lucky, A Cat
170	When The War Is Over, I Will Still Be Here
174	Me, Nikolai, A Mercenary
179	Run, Run, Run Away, Come Again Another Day
187	The Enduring Testament of Human Cruelty
190	A Lighthouse in Memory
197	Afterword—Bookstores in Taiwan
199	About the Author

A Letter from the Son of A Dissident to the Son of A Dissident

Dear Sabastian:

I am writing you this letter to share my experience of being the son of a political dissident. The purpose of this letter is to make repressed voices heard as loud as possible. They should resonate like thundering from the sky of high summer, the deafening heartbeats of the sacrificed, or echoes of foot shackles during a death march.

Before your father's arrest and the subsequent global rescue efforts, I had never followed news of him—even though your father's name was ubiquitous in the media. He was called a '"tycoon" due to his media group, fashion business, and real estate investments. I paid little attention to his empire, dismissing his publications as mere popular culture or tabloids. However, when the large-scale arrests began in Hong Kong, your father made a surprising decision: he refused to leave Hong Kong. At 73 years old upon his arrest, he now faces charges of "slanderous, derogatory remarks and attacks against Chinese leaders" under the National Security Law. It could result in his lifelong imprisonment.

Today, I am close to your father's age. When my father was arrested by the ruling power in Taiwan, he was about your age now. I was five when my father left. Although the formal story in my family was that he went to graduate school in the US, I always knew that wasn't the case. I don't remember if I knew it was a lie from the beginning or if I gradually realized my father wasn't in the US. First, graduate school doesn't take decades for any degree; second, the letters we sent to and received from him were not to or from the US. I did not know what my younger sister believed; I never asked her. I only knew that if I divulged my suspicion that my father wasn't in the US as Mom told us, both of them would be deeply hurt.

I had a puppy I called Freedom. Since my father's departure, I couldn't sleep well, and a friend of my parents suggested that my mother adopt a pet for me and my younger sister. Freedom slept with me, although Mom forbade him from being in any bed. I always allowed Freedom to share my bed after Mom retired to her bedroom. With Freedom, my sleep was much improved. Do you have pets, Sebastian?

Looking back, we all underestimated the cruelty of state violence. Dictatorship spares no free air for its people. Your father bravely resists the communist power, and ironically, my father was persecuted by an anti-communist regime during the Cold War.

My father was an English teacher. The books he published for English learning, including grammar, vocabulary, and practice tests, became the only income for my family. In this aspect, we were lucky compared to many other political prisoners whose families collapsed right after their imprisonment. Many of them encountered scams during their rescue attempts, and all the fortunes of their families were taken advantage of in their most vulnerable times. Although the assets your father possessed in Hong Kong have been frozen under the National Security Law, I suppose you and your family are still doing all right in terms of financial support, given your father's very successful entrepreneurship before his imprisonment and the assets your family owns outside of Hong Kong. On the other hand, it gives the regime a perfect excuse for the charge of "Collusion with Foreign Power."

In the tenth year of my father's imprisonment, my mother finally told us what had happened to him and where he really was. We were not surprised that he wasn't in the US, but we were very confused as to why he was deemed a public enemy. The terms "sedition," "subversion," and "treason" were beyond our comprehension.

Unlike you, who are no longer able to return to Hong Kong to visit your father, I visited mine several times, each time after very long and difficult journeys by train, bus, and boat. My memories of my father during these visits are so vague. After the nauseating rides, I only wished for the meeting with my father, behind the barred window and through a telephone in such an unkind atmosphere, to be over soon. It did end soon. Although it took us a whole day to arrive at the prison, each visit was allowed only 15 minutes, and then we had to spend another whole day traveling back home. At 15, I must have been considered old enough to understand the political calamity enshrouding my family, but I wasn't. Nightmares of us getting lost on the deserted island or drowning in the sea have haunted me to this day.

What we fear most, naturally, are the inhuman conditions in which our fathers have been imprisoned. Following the news regarding your father since his arrest, I know he was placed in solitary confinement at Stanley Prison. There, he is allowed to spend only about 50 minutes outdoors each day. Despite being outdoors, the space allotted to him is no larger than a basketball court for walking.

From the very rare photos taken by the Associated Press, he was seen holding a book and walking with his head held high. I was particularly struck by the black sandals he wore; they reminded me of my father's own worn footwear that he had used for years. A former billionaire and now a political dissident, your father's courage in facing such a sudden shift from a luxurious life to despair is truly admirable.

Freedom died when he was 14 years old. He was killed by bone cancer. All these years we shared a bed, he was growing big, and so was I. The single bed became really crowded. But after his death, I felt odd without Freedom kicking me in my dreams from time to time. I wrote to my father about Freedom's death, although my father never met him. He kindly replied to comfort me, "Let's never forget Freedom. He will never be forgotten as long as we always keep him in our minds."

Dear Sabastian, I wonder if you wished your father never had made the decision to stay in Hong Kong, instead of leaving for the UK, where he is a citizen. My father had no choice. Years after his release, when Martial Law was lifted and freedom of expression was finally restored, my father began to write his memoir. It revealed that he attempted to take his own life more than once. My mother thought of committing suicide, too. Even though our fathers' mishaps are 70 years apart, hopelessness is the major killer for political prisoners and their families. Outsiders, even if they have great empathy, are unlikely to figure out what torturous experience we face. That is the reason why I hope my letter is able to bring you some light. Your father's courage and your effort of rescue through all possible means are not gone without being noticed. I am also convinced that he represents hope for many silenced people living in fear.

I am proud of my father, and I know you are proud of your father, too. And I have no doubt that your father is proud of you. My best wishes to you and your family.

Dr. C. M. Ka

Originally published by *Little Fish Magazine*

June

> A day is vast,
> Until noon,
> Then it renews itself like a roaming god—
> broken in half, bewildering and
> anew
>
> –*Duality: Hirshfield Intervention*[1], Bob Black

When June was invited to the march by Heather, the first thing she thought was not about the purpose of the march, but which pair of shoes she should wear. She had just bought a pair of new heels and she really wanted to wear them for important events, especially when she was told that Eason, among other boys from the architecture department, also would be going.

The mary jane shoes were dark green with 2-inch

---

1 From Jane Hirshfield's *A Day Is Vast*: A day is vast./Until noon./Then it's over.

heels, a flower of the same color on each side where the buckle was. But they were mostly for looks, not really comfortable if one wanted to walk for a long time, they would make one's feet sore. June couldn't afford high-end shoes, and she bought this pair online without the chance to try them on first. June was not unsatisfied with them, with the money she paid, it was reasonable to have a fancy looking product of passable quality. Should she wear them? Would they impress Eason or other boys? How long were they going to walk?

June decided against wearing the new shoes eventually; she reckoned that if her feet were sore she might look funny when she walked, it wouldn't be cool. She had such a miserable experience more than once before. The streets in Hong Kong were not really easy to walk with high heels, she'd avoid getting herself in trouble with a bunch of her college classmates. June put on her sneakers and took off, hoping there would be occasions later for her shiny green mary jane.

As advised by Heather, June put on a black shirt and brought a simple canvas tote to carry a bottle of water and an umbrella. She took a little money with her, in case after the march they still wanted to hang out and dine or drink something together.

Since all the marchers wore black outfits, it took

them quite some time to find each other near the Hill Knoll Pavilion in Victoria Park. June was surprised there were so many people joining the march. Heather handed her a sign with a cuffed hand over the red background, the words said "No China Extradition". Then they began to move westward slowly, and Eason and Jushua joined them when they walked toward Hennessy Road. It was almost four o'clock in the afternoon.

Joshua took out rice balls for them. The seaweed slices wrapping the rice had been slightly dampened after being put away in the fridge for a few hours, but they devoured them anyway. June had hoped that they could have a meal together later at night, but with so many people still joined in, the march seemed to be lasting forever.

It was a very well organized march, along their route June saw many first aid stations with Red Cross signs. And there were more spots providing drinking water. Did the event organizers expect to have a long day? The parade grew bigger and bigger. Speakers on soap boxes shouted the reasons why indicted offenders in Hong Kong should not be extradited to the Chinese mainland. Not until that point did June realize that the new law was not really about the trials of criminals but a tool to be used against Hong Kong political dissidents.

June heard several people arguing about the Umbrella Revolution, one of them insisted that it was a very successful movement, and another mocked, "If it was a success, why are we still here today?"

"Without the Umbrella Revolution, we would be in a worse situation. At least we are still able to express our thoughts today."

"True. But my old man believes that we are causing trouble…"

"Don't you see? They are the troubles. Their belief in law and orders is totally illusional, that's the problem. They don't rebel, no matter how unjustified the law and order becomes…"

Heather and Eason were also discussing the disagreements and conflicts between different groups that had participated in previous movements. June listened, she had no idea that Heather had been so involved in these movements, and the same was true for Eason. June wished to take part in their conversation, but she was not very clear about the issues concerning them. Would Eason be impressed by Heather more, instead of June? Heather was a plump girl, her charm came from her eloquence in public affairs. June was slender and very careful about her style, but today she felt the dress code of wearing black erased her opportunity to stand out.

What a pity.

"The Umbrella Movement was our wake-up-call!" The same guy insisting that the Movement was a success said hopefully. But an older voice replied in a cold tone, "Hong Kong people should have been woken up as early as the Tiananmen Slaughter, but the majority never learned the lesson."

"You can't wake a person who is pretending to be asleep." Another person said in a regrettable tone.

Ding! It was a notification of text from June's mobile phone. June checked it, "You are not in the march, are you?" It was her mom. June put her phone back in her tote. Seeing people in black shirts keep coming into the procession, June suspected that the entire population of people in their twenties was on the streets, and her mother's question seemed to be so ridiculous. June reckoned that the march would be a hot topic in school on the coming Monday, and she certainly did not want to be left out.

June was born in 1997, the year that Hong Kong was handed over to China from the UK. In the same year there were sixty-three thousand babies born in Hong Kong, an unusual generation in an unusual time. When June was six, Hong Kong was hit by SARS, a mysterious disease of the respiratory system transmitted by the novel coronavirus, resulting in the cancellation of her kindergarten graduation ceremony. In 2008, when she was eleven, the Olympic Games were staged in Beijing. Since that time, her parents, among many adults who grew up under the UK system, began to feel they were more Chinese than British. In the same year, Hong Kong was in the epicenter of the global financial crisis. And in 2009, the entire Hong Kong region was devastated by Swine Flu, and yes, it was an epidemic involving humans, so June missed her elementary graduation ceremony again. When the Umbrella Revolution was happening in 2014, and the streets and public spaces were occupied by protestors for eighty days, June was restrained by her parents from participating in it. June was only seventeen years-old at that time, not even a voter yet, and was engaged in all kinds of examinations in high school, she really did not pay much attention to the matters of direct elections or being represented by a few people. Even today, June was not very clear why the extradition of offenders to China was such an essential issue.

Obviously it was, otherwise there couldn't be so many people taking to the streets to protest, and there wouldn't be such great and forceful opposition from the law to stop them.

They began seeing law enforcement moving

around them, some of them were in uniforms that indicated they had never even seen Hong Kong before. The marchers moved on, shouting slogans and singing, but the troops from unknown origins certainly changed the cheerful atmosphere right as they had just taken off. Joshua got a message that on Lung Wo Road the police had begun to throw tear gas at marchers, so they started to shout "withdraw the police" in unison again and again. From where they were, the shouting was heard from groups near and far, from bridges or from buildings surrounding them. It irritated the law enforcement even more, and one band of police in black helmets, black bulletproof vests and black batons marched toward them with black shields. Involuntarily they recoiled, but boys stood before girls.

Four or five protestors from another direction ran behind the armed police troops and shouted on the top of their lungs, attempting to distract them. Several policemen did turn and run after these protestors, but most of the policemen were still marching toward June's group step by step. Unexpectedly, a person behind June threw a water bottle at the police. When they still had no idea how to respond to the situation, four or five policemen rushed toward their group and disbanded them. They spotted the bottle thrower and surrounded him, and as the guy had no way to run, they hit him hard with their batons. The guy squatted down and held his arms to protect his head, but the policemen began to kick his sides and back with their heavy boots. Seeing this, Eason tried to break up the beating, but immediately he was surrounded, too. And as other protestors approached to help their fellow protestors, they were expelled by the rest of the police troops. June was surprised to see more policemen had come, and they moved quickly. In no time, their group had been downsized to no more than a dozen protesters.

Outside of their circle, other protesters continued shouting "We have the right for non-violent demonstration! Non-violence! Withdraw the police!" But their sounds were further and further away, June assumed that they were pushed away, and now she and her friends were really isolated.

They were ordered to lie down on their stomach with their hands on their back head. They were beaten up when they followed the order slowly, not to mention resistance. June felt that her tote was brutally dragged away, which carried her mobile phone, drinking water, purse and an umbrella. Then one by one they were handcuffed and thrown into a police truck like pigs to be slaughtered.

They were not allowed to speak in the truck, and with hands cuffed, they could only worm little by little from the weight of someone else's body. They had no idea where they were sent to, the truck must be driven through quite bumpy roads, and June felt she would throw up any time.

It was a hot day, they could feel the body heat from one another, they could smell each other's breath. June was not sure if Heather, Eason and Jushua were also in the truck or not. She hoped they were, and at the same time she hoped they were not.

***

A shrieking song sung out in a female voice echoed in June's head, it had to be from a street theater nearby. It was a line from an ancient story, the heroine was weeping in the most ferocious and accusing tone. A woman, Dou-Er, was wronged to be the murderer of her bullyer but couldn't claim her justice because of the corrupt local officials. Before her execution, Dou-Er pointed to the sky and swore her innocence; she cursed that a storm after a long drought would avenge her. After her death, in the third year of the drought, a snow storm in midsummer hit the place bringing devastation.

June has no idea where she was and how long she had been in this horrifying place. She had fallen asleep in a chair, pain and soreness pervaded her body. The concrete building must have been abandoned for a long time, foul smells of mildew and rotten things made her so sick when she was dragged into this dim cell. But after a long time, not knowing how long, June began to feel her own breath turning bad after not eating and drinking at all for so long. Her lips were parched, her eyelids were heavy. Her shoulders and hips were aching first, then the pain became burning, and gradually her limbs went numb. If the floor weren't so dirty with puddles of still water and circled by mosquitoes, June would lie down to rest, instead of sitting in the chair.

Policemen and policewomen had come and gone several times, June did not remember how many times. Each time they showed up they used all kinds of humiliating words to her, calling her a parasite, a cockroach, among other names of loathsome bugs. At first June tried to explain that she did not do anything except walk in the march, and she had no intention to violate the peace the marchers had promised. But she was not listened to. The police did not care about her explanation. One time they brought a paper and forced June to sign on it, which was her "self-statement" with her "confession" that she had participated in the conspiracy of agitating the "riots". June was shocked by the wording; a peaceful march demanding for the fundamental autonomy of Hong Kong's jurisdiction was interpreted as a riot?! And as one of the supporters of hundreds of thousands, she had become an agitator?! June was not even clear about the purpose of the demonstration when she started walking with the others.

Was Heather an agitator, too? Was Eason as well? And Joshua? June wanted to cry, but her body was too dry to shed any tears.

Had her mom called her again? Did her family know where she was? Recalling that not so long ago she was still thinking of impressing boys with her new shoes, June felt so bitter and hopeless. When would she be going home to see her family? When would she be in school again?

The door opened again, and a policewoman entered, followed by a policeman.

"What to charge for this one?" The policeman asked. June was identified as "this one".

"Obstruction of justice." The policewoman said.

Hearing it, June's helplessness suddenly and unexpectedly changed to anger. She gathered all her energy left and stared at the two people who planned to frame her with crimes she never committed. June's eyesight must be full of resentment and contempt, because in a flash of a moment, they were betrayed by their surprise. But they maintained a composed demeanor, in a cruel way. The policeman wrote down something on his pad and both of them took off.

Yes, no doubt I just have obstructed justice with my eyes, June thought to herself. Their justice, which is as disgusting as the filthy puddles in the smelly cell.

Originally published by *Olney Magazine*

Endangered Youth

Freedom, I was told, is nothing but the distance between the hunter and its prey.
 ~Ocean Vuong, *On Earth, We're Briefly Gorgeous*

1970, Court Judgment, Taiwan Garrison Command

Lin Shui-Chuan, 34 years old
Occupation: Taipei City Councilor
Attempting to subvert the government with unlawful means
Sentenced to 15 years of imprisonment, 10 years of disenchantment of civil rights

Chang Ming-Zhan, 29 years old
Occupation: Librarian
Attempting to subvert the government with unlawful means
Sentenced to 12 years of imprisonment, 10 years

of disenchantment of civil rights
Lin Dao-Ping, 26 years old
Occupation: Medical school student, National Taiwan University
Attempting to subvert the government with unlawful means
Sentenced to 8 years of imprisonment, 5 years of disenchantment of civil rights

Findings

Defendant Lin Shui-Chuan had violated the Anti-Hoodlum Law in 1961, by agitating people with ideas against social stability and harmony. Dissatisfied with reality and without repentance, Lin Shui-Chuan decided to instigate the independent status of Taiwan from the Republic of China with Chang Ming-Zhan and Lin Dao-Ping. In April, 1965, the three defendants gathered in White Cloud Villa in Taipei, they became sworn brothers and initiated a plan for Taiwan's autonomy. In summer of the same year, the defendants were joined by LC, LS and CC at the Jade Mountain Inn in Taipei to discuss the affairs of Taiwan's independence. In October, LS went to Japan to meet separatists hiding overseas and was told to use "Harajuku" (meadow lodging) as their secret password for their meetings. They contacted one another through mails between

Taiwan and Japan which were written in Chinese, Japanese, or English in secret codes.

The defendants and others also met in the Black Beauty Night Club in Taipei from time to time and exchanged information about their progress in Taiwan and Japan. In the Club, they drafted pamphlets that incited people to overturn the government and establish the Taiwan Republic. Later the pamphlets were printed and mailed to students of the law school from the National Taiwan University and people in the surrounding neighborhoods. The defendants assigned LC and a new member YI to print handouts of "Taiwan Autonomy and A New Government", the defendants told LC and YI that they would be funding the expense of making the handouts. The handouts were made and given away around Nanjing E. Rd. in Taipei.

In August 1966, the defendants were given 30 copies of "Independent Taiwan", a publication issued from Japan. They began to distribute the publication secretly and initiated a plan to publish a newsletter "Frontier" to spread their ideas of separatism in Taiwan. In November, the defendants met LC, YI, WW, LD and CK (who had turned himself in later) at the Taipei Municipal Library. Their meeting was under the disguise of a book club to cover their activities for Taiwan's independence. On this occasion they founded Taiwan Youth Union and elected Chang Ming-Zhan as its general secretary. A bylaw was drafted for the Union as well. Later the defendants invited YI, WW and CK to Songshan Inn to talk about how to purchase explosives to bomb symbolic buildings and assassinate governmental officials. CK expressed his disagreement with taking violent measures. No conclusion had been reached during the meeting in the Songshan Inn. In the same evening, after the farewell dinner for YI, a graduate of the National Taiwan University who was going to Japan for his graduate study, they went to a hot spring in Wulai and stayed at the Emerald Mountain Inn for the night. In the Emerald Mountain Inn, they drafted the manifesto of the Taiwan Youth Union and bid YI to publish it once he arrived in Japan.

In December, 1966 and January, 1967, the defendants and others had frequent meetings on different occasions, they secretly drafted a constitutional law and the organizational chart of the new government, including a congress, for the new nation. They also discussed whether they should produce handouts for the memorial day of 228 Incident[1] or not. Around that time, activities for the in-

---

1 On Feb 28, 1947, clashes occurred between Taiwanese

dependence of Taiwan became very active in Japan. Separatists there not only remotely organized actions in Taiwan, they also raised money from Taiwanese businessmen in Japan and Japanese sympathizers of Taiwan's independence movement. From the materials found in the office of the Taiwan Youth Union, several of its members had plans to destroy bridges, reservoirs or oil refineries throughout Taiwan, among other important infrastructure. But the defendants denied there were such plans, and there is no evidence showing the defendants were involved in such plans. There were documents found showing that in a meeting about assisination of government officials, the defendants were present. The defendants were arrested by the Investigation Bureau in May, 1967 before they could start their actions.

Reasoning

Taiwan was returned to the Republic of China from Japan in 1945, and has not only freed itself from colonizers' oppression but also witnessed long-term prosperity and development. Under the gov-

---

people and the ruling Nationalist Party that just took over Taiwan from Japan, resulting in brutal military oppression. The Nationalist government did not rectify the conflicts, instead, it imposed Martial Law, followed by the long period of White Terror.

ernance of the Nationalist Party, Taiwan is enjoying the benefits of fast economic growth and development. In all circumstances, Taiwan is always an inseparable part of the Republic of China and should co-shoulder the responsibilities of anti-communism and for the great goal of recovering mainland China (the false regime of the People's Republic of China) in order to liberate the society from brutal communist rule. The defendants' criticism of the government, such as its corruption, repression of local culture, or negligence of human rights are groundless, undoubtedly the ruling party is a government of integrity and justified to rule. The defendants' desire to build up a new nation, an independent Taiwan, has damaged the social harmony and people's trust in the government. Their attempts to weaken or to jeopardize the power of the Republic of China by violence is not to be tolerated.

Conclusion

The sentences of the three defendants are according to the Articles 173, 174 and 175 of Martial Law, and Subarticle 1, Article 2 of the Betrayers Punishment Act, Article 9 of the Espionage Law, Subarticle 1 & 2, Article 8 of the Anti-Insurgency Law, and Article 11, Subarticle 2 of Article 37, Article 59 of the Criminal Law.

***

2021, Hong Kong District Court
Joshua Hwang, 24 years old
Occupation: Secretary-general of Demosista (now disbanded)
Organizing assembly unlawfully
4 years of imprisonment

Nathan Lao, 27 years old
Occupation: Legislator of Hong Kong Island
Former secretary-general of students' union of the Lingnan University
Organizing assembly unlawfully
3 years and 8 months of imprisonment

Alex Chou, 30 years old
Occupation: Graduate student of the London School of Economy and Political Science
Organizing assembly unlawfully
2 years and 7 months of imprisonment

Findings

On Sept 26, 2014, Joshua Hwang, Alex Chou and Nathan Lao (the defendants), in the action of "Occupy Central" or "Umbrella Movement", jumped over the building fence of the Hong Kong

Government to occupy the Civic Square and were followed by hundreds of students. Their law-breaking behavior triggered a series of sit-ins in the center of the city, causing tremendous inconvenience to other people. The protestors demanded direct election of the Chief Executive of the Hong Kong Special Territory, and their protests lasted for more than two months until the law enforcement expelled them in December. During this time, governmental buildings and public spaces were vandalized, shops were looted, and transportation was paralyzed. As a financial hub of Asia, Hong Kong's daily operation was disrupted.

"Occupy Central" had caused huge losses and great sufferings to the people of Hong Kong. It not only jeopardized the peace of the society, harmed Hong Kong's economic activities, but also soiled Hong Kong's reputation as an open, thriving and livable city. The so-called Umbrella Revolution also sent a warning message implying the possible rise of anarchy, or the very dangerous ideas of separatism—Hong Kong's independence.

In recent years, an unhealthy trend in Hong Kong has been detected that certain people engaged in illegal activities with the excuse of exercising their rights of freedom of expression. These rebellious events included the agenda "Disobey the Laws to

Achieve Justice", which greatly excited youth whose thinking was still immature to disrespect law and order. The defendants, at that time still in a tender age, were undoubtedly influenced by such contempt of law.

It is reasonable to assume that the movement is not entirely a domestic movement, as external forces are involved. Only happening half a year before Occupy Central, the Sunflower Student Movement in Taiwan set a very bad example of young people occupying the congress and blackmailing the government against having further economic ties with China. Undoubtedly, anti-China agitators from Taiwan had provided protestors in Hong Kong with instructions on how to dodge law and order, and supplied illegal tools under the excuse of establishing a civil society.

There is also evidence showing forces behind the protestors from the UK and the US, the tear-gas-proof masks and pepper-spray-proof gear they carried were examples. It is also reasonable to assume that the UK still desires to impose its influence over its former colony. And the US, once threatening to terminate Hong Kong's "special trading status", never conceals its ambition to replace China's leading economic position by taking advantage of the turmoil in Hong Kong.

During and after the illegal "Occupy Movement" in 2014, 993 persons were arrested for offenses of unlawful assembly, possession of offensive weapons, assaults, assaulting police officers, theft, vandalism, criminal intimidation and possession of unapproved drugs etc. Among them, 216 persons had undergone judicial proceedings, 116 persons were prosecuted, and 42 were convicted. The defendants were prosecuted for inciting unlawful assembly in accordance with the Public Order Ordinance.

Reasoning

Although the Basic Law and the Bill of Rights Ordinance endow Hong Kong public freedom of assembly and speech, including demonstration, the freedom is not without conditions. Any anti-government remarks of secession, subversion, or terrorism, or collusion with foreign powers that will result in the society plunging into chaos should be restricted, and people making such remarks or taking such actions are committing crimes. Criminals should be sanctioned by the law.

Thanks to the newly implemented National Security Law, over the past years, several organizations including Demosista (founded by the defendants), Amnesty International Hong Kong, student union of the Chinese University of Hong Kong, China

Human Rights Lawyers Concern Group and a group called Student Politicism, among many others, had been dismissed due to their incorrect political attitudes. News outlets such as the Stand News, Citizen News, Apple Daily, Post 852 and Mad Dog Daily that often distorted and vilified government messages were also dissolved after the sedition investigation.

When expressing one's opinions, one must abide by the law; once any violation of public safety occurs, the police are responsible to enforce social order. During the trial, the law enforcement officials fulfilled their duty of presenting all the evidence of the offenses. This court strongly condemns violent actions for any political demand and is obliged to restore social stability. The penalties this court is handing down are according to its power defined by the judicial and legislative bodies of the Hong Kong Special Territory.

The conviction and sentences to the three defendants were not because of their political agenda, but because of their violations of law and order, and their intentional destruction of social harmony.

Conclusion

The court decision is based on the Section 18(1) of the Public Order Ordinance, and the Section

81C(1) of the Criminal Procedure Ordinance

Author's Note:

The strident National Security Law was implemented in Hong Kong by China in 2020. It tremendously tightens political control and censorship, and its persecution of dissidents by framing them in involvement of violence is appallingly similar to that of Taiwan half century ago.

Grandpa Fu's Suitcase

Following Grandpa Fu's funeral, his children took the necessary steps to prepare the house for sale, because none of his three children lived in Taiwan. Relatives were invited to inspect his belongings, including a desk, two chairs, a bookshelf filled with books, and a pair of leather shoes that he had only worn a handful of times. In addition, a few inexpensive trinkets from Grandpa Fu's collection were also given away.

They found that beneath Grandpa Fu's bed lay a suitcase made from genuine leather and sewn with sturdy thread. In the case, they discovered a meticulously crafted interior of durable fabric that concealed the leather seams. Nestled inside was a dark gray suit, untouched and never before seen on Grandpa. Though it was slightly mildewed, its delicate texture still could be appreciated by touch. Alongside the suit lay a first-aid kit, a water bottle, and a pack of dehydrated food that had expired around the time before Grandpa Fu fell ill. In addition, there were provisions for personal hygiene, including a toothbrush, a small tube of toothpaste, a clean towel, fresh underwear, and a pair of new socks.

Under everything else lay a photo of Grandpa Fu's parents. The image was so faded and brittle that it threatened to crumble at the slightest touch.

Obviously the suitcase was Grandpa Fu's preparation in case he had to embark on a hurried trip with very short notice. Grandpa Fu moved to Taiwan in 1949, he was a soldier first, then a refugee, then his prolonged exile made him one of the millions of the Chinese diaspora.

All the relatives witnessing the revelation of Grandpa Fu's secret suitcase were bewildered. Did he still believe he was going home to China? The dried food was still good a couple of years ago, Grandpa Fu wouldn't still expect to return after more than seventy years of the civil war. Grandpa Fu was never affected by dementia or delusion, his mind remained clear even his frail body betrayed his strong mind during his last days.

Grandpa Fu's eldest son Ming-Cheng carefully retrieved the pictures of his grandparents whom he had never met. He brought them to a photo development business for digital repair and ordered several copies of the digitally restored photos for his brother and sister, and his own children.

Ming-Cheng went to study in the US after completing his college education in Taiwan and fulfilling his mandatory military service. He pursued a degree in information technology because he was advised that this profession had the highest likelihood of providing opportunities for foreigners to settle down in the US. Following in his footsteps, Ming-Cheng's brother, Ming-Chih, also moved to the US several years later. Ming-Chih's expertise was in biotech and pharmacy, which were highly sought after in the US during the 1990s. Meanwhile, their younger sister, Ming-Jen, went to Japan, where she became an interpreter of Chinese-Japanese languages for diplomats.

The three siblings hardly had any chance to reunite, they usually took turns to visit their parents in Taiwan. Even though both of the brothers were living in the US, one was in Chicago, another in San Francisco, they also rarely met. After their mother's passing, the siblings hired a caretaker to prepare meals for Grandpa Fu and ensured he received medical attention and renewed his prescription medications. Ming-Cheng was aware that he and his siblings faced criticism for being absent during their parents' old age and illness. However, in their fifties, their careers were demanding, making it extremely challenging for them to take time off from their jobs.

Around twenty years ago, Ming-Chih was offered a position in a prestigious institute of research and development in Taiwan, when Taiwan's government was investing in the rising industry of life science. Ming-Chih had seriously considered moving back to Taiwan with his family, but Grandpa Fu was against it. He told Ming-Chih the education in the US was better for his children.

Ming-Jen took their father's suit to a dry cleaning service as she planned to bring it with her to Japan, wanting to keep it as a lasting memory of her father. Why did their family members end up so far apart from each other? Upon reflecting on their situation Ming-Cheng realized that his family was just one among many in Taiwan whose members had dispersed. They had spent limited time with their parents during their adult lives, and their children had little knowledge of their grandparents.

While the three siblings were asking around which columbarium they should shrine their parents' ashes, a relative told them they should bring it to the US, "Taiwan might be at war soon. It's safer to bring it with you."

As Ming-Cheng touched the meticulously

crafted leather suitcase, a sudden realization struck him—they had never truly escaped their identity as refugees. It was Grandpa Fu's decision that all his children should leave Taiwan as soon as they reached adulthood, recognizing the ongoing threat of war looming across the strait. Now, memories resurfaced of his father obtaining his first car through loans when they were teenagers. One thing that puzzled him was his father's habit of keeping a full tank of gasoline, even after a short ride that barely consumed a quarter of it.

Grandpa Fu was constantly prepared for the possibility of being on the run once more. The experience of fleeing from China to Taiwan had surely left deep scars of trauma within him, and he wanted to ensure his family would be better equipped if a similar situation arose. However, on such a small island, where could they possibly escape to? Naturally, he made the decision to send his children away to places he deemed least likely to be engulfed in war.

Although Ming-Cheng and Ming-Chih had scholarships or tuition-free for their graduate studies in the US, it was still very challenging for his parents to support their lives in the very expensive US. Their father worked as a middle level public employer and their mother earned some income by a home assembly for small toy manufacturers. They lived in a very cramped apartment, almost never traveled, and hardly dined out. Every penny they earned, they saved for their children's studies overseas. During the summers they used the air-conditioner sparingly, and as the old apartment really needed remodeling, they repaired everything with their own hands. When a high-rise building was constructed next to their humble dwelling, they considered it a blessing as it provided cooler summers. When their children started working and began to have savings, they offered choices that they could buy a newer apartment or have their apartment remodeled, but Grandpa Fu told them they should invest the money into the education of their children, instead of on the living of two old people since there wouldn't be many years left for them. Ming-Cheng assumed that it was difficult for older people to make big changes.

Even in his old age, Grandpa Fu still had the nightmares of fleeing from war. The water bottle, the dried food, and the fine suit he packed in his suitcase were for a dignified escape. But where could he run to? Ming-Cheng looked around the place their parents spent five or six decades of their lives, thinking almost nothing but to provide their children and grandchildren safety and peace. He recalled the inquiries he received from colleagues and neighbors in Chicago, questioning the safety of traveling to

Taiwan due to escalating tensions across the strait. It dawned on him that, throughout their lives, they had never truly shed their refugee identity.

It must be tough to be on the run all his father's life, Ming-Cheng thought. When could they stop fleeing? Ming-Cheng seriously considered the idea that perhaps he and his brother and sister should maintain this apartment, and when he retired he could move back; if war did not happen.

Originally published by *The Seraphic Review*

Grandpa Fu's Roommate

Grandpa Fu wasn't a particularly good storyteller, almost all the stories impressing us he ever told were about Ah-Chuan, his friend in youth. What was unusual about Ah-Chuan? Ah-Chuan was unlike anyone Grandpa Fu had ever known. According to Grandpa Fu's stories, Ah-Chuan was a man of many talents and endless curiosity. First, Ah-Chuan was a Sci-Fi writer, he wrote wonderful stories about outer space, he wove tales of distant galaxies through fantastical adventures. We were somewhat surprised that Grandpa Fu, an old school man, would appreciate the genre of Sci-Fi. But when we looked up Ah-Chuan's formal name, Lai Yu-Chuan, and any fiction about outer space of his time, we found nothing related to Ah-Chuan or Lai Yu-Chuan. Perhaps he used a pen name? Sci-Fi was a relatively new genre in the 1950s even in the West, not to mention in Taiwan.

And while the puzzle was not solved yet, Ah-

Chuan's identity was changed again. This time Ah-Chuan became a brilliant astronaut working for NASA, unraveling the mysteries of the cosmos. We tried to trick Grandpa Fu to talk more about NASA, he admitted that he knew very little about NASA, "Wait until Ah-Chuan comes back, I will ask what had happened over all these years."

Amidst all the inconsistent details of Ah-Chuan's life stories, there was some background information of Ah-Chuan never changed, such as he was from Kaohsiung, he majored in English literature in the Taiwan Provincial Teachers' College, which was where Grandpa Fu met Ah-Chuan. Grandpa Fu majored in Chemistry, but they were roommates of the student dormitory.

And in another time Ah-Chuan was an actor. What? What did he play? He played Lawrence in Arabia, Anton Chekhov, and China's last emperor... he acted in a lot of roles. Did he act as an astronaut? No, at that time there were no astronauts. We told ourselves that Ah-Chuan was Grandpa Fu's imaginary friend, because when a person gets old, he would become a child again.

***

Lai Yu-Chuan was my first close Taiwanese friend.

I am from Mainland China; I came to Taiwan with my parents after the Communist insurgents raged and occupied the whole of China. My father worked for the government, so we could settle down in Mid-Taiwan and resume our life in the provincial capital. After months of study, I was luckily admitted to Taiwan Provincial Teachers' College in Taipei, majoring in Chemistry, a subject I had begun before we were forced to leave our hometown in China.

Lai Yu-Chuan called himself Ah-Chuan, so we also referred to him as Ah-Chuan. He was in the Department of English Literature, so many of his books were in English. However, to my surprise, the books he carried with him most of the time were not by Shakespeare, but rather science fiction. He had magazines with very colorful and figurative covers, like *Astounding Stories of Super Science* from America. He said his relatives in Japan bought them from American soldiers. Ah-Chuan was particularly excited about those stories set in other galaxies.

"What? There are humans living on other planets? That is impossible," I expressed my doubt.

Ah-Chuan just smiled, "It's fictional. But who knows?"

"It's called science fiction, but it's not scientific."

However, when Ah-Chuan interpreted the stories in our dormitory room, we were all infatuated.

"One day, humans will really be traveling in outer space," he said with great confidence.

***

When Grandpa Fu was 83 years old, he suffered a stroke. Whenever we had time, we spent it accompanying him for his rehab. For a man in his eighties, his recovery was not bad, but slow. It could be frustrating, for him and for all of us. Grandpa Fu stopped telling us Ah-Chuan's stories, whether he was an astronaut or a Sci-Fi writer, or an actor, or any imaginative identity.

One time when we felt exhausted trying to help Grandpa Fu walk, I thought it might be clever to ask him, "Do you wish Ah-Chuan to visit you?"

Grandpa Fu blinked his eyes, then he turned his head away to the dimming sun glow in the rehabilitation center of the hospital. After several moments that felt as long as a century, Grandpa Fu said without turning his head back, "He never returned. My roommate never returned. Ah-Chuan never returned." Then Grandpa Fu began to cry, his effort to repress his agitation made his silent choking even more miserable, and we were stunned. What a stupid question I had asked. Ever since that time, Ah-Chuan completely disappeared between Grandpa and us, no one dared to mention his name again.

***

The night in early summer of our last year in college was the last time I saw Ah-Chuan. I was already in bed in the dormitory when Ah-Chuan unexpectedly came back. He had been away much of the time; at first, I thought Ah-Chuan went home every month, sometimes more than once a month. Later, I realized Ah-Chuan was very active in various affairs; he was a contributor to a newspaper's supplement and organized book readings from time to time. From our other roommates, I learned that some of the books were very sensitive. Before the Communist Party took over China, Ah-Chuan had contacts there for literary exchanges. I knew Ah-Chuan was deeply interested in modernism; he even organized a writer group for it. However, all communication between Taiwan and China had been banned since we moved to Taiwan, and any contact with people there, regardless of the purpose, was a violation of the law.

The student protests a couple of months ago turned out to be related to the ban, many students having connections with people in China were in trouble. I knew Ah-Chuan participated in many protests, he criticized the corruption of the new government. My father also worked for the government, but he worked really hard, so I did not know why Ah-Chuan and his fellow protestors thought the government was bad.

I suspected that Ah-Chuan never really stopped contacting his friends in China, he did it secretly and eventually ran into trouble. That night he asked me not to turn on the light and he hurriedly packed several things before taking off again. I kept asking where he was going, but he never answered me.

"If anyone comes looking for me, just tell them I never came back. I never showed up!" In the dimness of our dormitory, Ah-Chuan's bloodless face looked like a ghost. Sensing something really bad was happening, I quickly retrieved the scholarship money I had just received and handed it to him. At first Ah-Chuan was going to decline my offer, but after thinking for a second, he accepted it and said determinedly, "I will return it as soon as possible."

After Ah-Chuan's departure, I nervously practiced his request, telling anyone looking for him, "Ah-Chuan never returned. Ah-Chuan never returned! My roommate never returned!"

I noticed I was trembling, it made me even more suspicious for being lying. Fortunately, no one came.

***

Without Ah-Chuan in Grandpa Fu's life, we had very few topics to share. I was bewildered as to why Grandpa's imaginary friend had transformed from a figure that greatly cheered him up to one that greatly upset him. I couldn't ask.

Grandpa became less and less active, both physically and mentally. He only wished to go outdoors on sunny days, but even when he was pushed to a park in the sunlight, he did not interact with anyone or the environment. He sat in his wheelchair, his mind seemingly lost in the past.

***

After the suspension of classes, I returned to school. My mother had opposed my return, considering the turmoil caused by the student protests and the consequential arrests. She feared I might get involved too. But my father believed that the government had quelled the chaos, and I should certainly continue my studies. Still, before I left, he gravely warned me, "Don't get involved with those agitators; they are hired by the Communist Party, using students as a disguise."

I also wanted to go back to school to see if

Ah-Chuan was all right. But he never appeared. Throughout the whole semester, the upper bunk of my bed remained empty. I didn't know where I could get information about Ah-Chuan's whereabouts, and in fact, I didn't dare to ask around.

As the end of my last semester in college approached, I began to pack my things and mail some of my books home. Looking around the room that had been my home for four years, and seeing Ah-Chuan's untouched belongings, I couldn't resist opening the drawer of his desk. There wasn't anything special inside. Like every young man of our age, his things were disorganized; he just randomly threw things in there—notebooks, pens, letters, and some stationery.

On a pile of writing paper, I found Ah-Chuan's handwritten poem:

When the piercing dart finds my heart,
My soul, unbound, prepares for distant shores.
To realms unseen, where stars in rapture play,
In endless dance, they hold an eternal wave.
With whispered words of grace, I bid farewell,
To soar beyond, where dreams and truths ensue.
Though earthly bounds may falter and decay,
My essence lives, in hearts that love's light sway.
And 'tis I, amidst the starry gleam,

In cosmic seas, where dreams and visions teem.
For in that boundless expanse, wild and free,
My spirit roams, in timeless reverie.

I never understood poetry, but Ah-Chuan's words looked so beautiful to me. I took it and pressed the paper by inserting it into one of my textbooks, thinking I would return it when Ah-Chuan came back.

I never heard from Ah-Chuan again. I prayed that he had escaped capture and run far away. Ah-Chuan was such a talented person; he would be successful in whatever endeavor he pursued. I wished he could travel to the other galaxy as he always told us, decades ago, it was possible.

***

Later we moved to different cities for studies or for work, we saw Grandpa Fu much less, and he passed away three years after his stroke.

Sixty years after Grandpa Fu's graduation from the teachers college, our youngest brother Lun-Hsiun enrolled in it, the campus having become a university of education. For spring break, Lun-Hsiun went home and showed us a photo he took from an exhibition held in the university's library: April 6

Incident in 1949. In the picture was a young man in a prisoner's uniform with his name stitched over his shirt chest. The name gave me a twitch of heart, "Lai Yu-Chuan".

"Google it," Lun-Hsiun said, and obviously he had done so.

I took my mobile phone and typed Ah-Chuan's full name, the same photo Lun-Hsiun took jumped up, with text provided by the Committee for Transitional Justice:

> Lai Yu-Chuan (1929-1950), a native of Kaohsiung City. He enrolled in the Department of English Literature at Taiwan Provincial Teachers' College.
>
> In November 1947, he was introduced to the underground organization of the Communist Party of China by his classmate Chen Shui-Mu. In September 1948, he participated in a branch meeting of the Teachers' College and served as a propaganda officer. During his time at school, he was mainly involved in activities such as the food committee, drama club, and consumer cooperatives.
>
> Lai Yu-Chuan was also a frequent contributor of the "Bridge", supplement of Taiwan Shin Sheng News Daily. He published poetry and

fiction, as well as essays campaigning for the exchange between modern Taiwanese and Chinese literature, especially the emerging genre of Sci-Fi.

In early May 1950, after the arrest of leading cadres of the Chinese Communist Party, Lai Yu-Chuan was arrested at his home in Kaohsiung. In September, the Taiwan Provincial Security Command sentenced him to life imprisonment and deprivation of civil rights for life on charges of "conspiring to subvert the government by illegal means." However, President Chiang Kai-Shek ordered a change in the verdict to the death penalty. On November 29, Lai Yu-Chuan was executed by the Fourth Military Police Regiment. He was 21 years old.

"What the hell?" was my first response. No doubt this Lai Yu-Chuan was Ah-Chuan, Grandpa Fu's imaginary friend. They were about the same age, and studied at the teachers' college about the same years. They shared the same room in the student dormitory. Ah-Chuan was not really an astronaut, nor an actor, nor a Sci-Fi writer, he had no time to become any of them, although in his very short lifetime he had been exposed to these fields and accomplished as much as a young person could have.

Years went by, more and more secret archives

from the White Terror period were released and digitized. Wronged cases were reinvestigated and studied, giving us a better perspective on what really could have happened during the large-scale arrests and student resistance. I often wondered, did Ah-Chuan try to recruit Grandpa Fu into the Communist Party? Was Grandpa Fu also a member? On the other hand, didn't Grandpa Fu and his parents end up in Taiwan because of the disasters caused by the Communist Party in China? However, according to the disclosed documents, many arrests, detentions, interrogations, and unlawful trials went beyond the purge of the communists; they targeted students protesting governmental corruption at the time. There were also victims from the same background as Grandpa Fu, so how close was Grandpa to becoming one of the many victims?

Most of all, did Grandpa Fu know Ah-Chuan was dead at all? Why did he make up all the stories about Ah-Chuan?

From the unearthed photo of Lai Yu-Chuan, one could see that his hands were tied at the back. It was taken right before his execution. 21-years-old in 1950, this image probably was one of the few for a young person at that time. Was he afraid? Did he regret what he had done? What he and his family had been through all these years? I realized I also began to make up stories about Ah-Chuan. What would he have become if he hadn't been killed?

"Ah-Chuan never returned. My roommate never returned!" Grandpa Fu's hoarse voice echoed in my head. I gathered that Grandpa Fu must have known Ah-Chuan was dead, otherwise he'd have found his old roommate and told him he was all right. Not wanting to end Ah-Chuan's life in his memory, Grandpa Fu revitalized Ah-Chuan with all kinds of best wishes he had for him, a successful Sci-Fi writer, actor, or astronaut. And it was definitely a good thing Grandpa Fu had done, because Ah-Chuan lived on in our minds for a much longer time than he really did, sharing the joys and sorrows of his life, as well as the legacy he left us.

Author's Note:

The April 6 incident in Taiwan originated from the arrest of two students in March, 1949, for alleged traffic violations, sparking protests with hundreds of students.
The regime of Chinese Nationalist Party, then engaged in the civil war with the underground Chinese Communist Party, asserted that the protests were instigated by CCP members. Consequently, on April 6, 1949, police and military forces were ordered to enter the campuses to quell the students. Hundreds of students were arrested, and unknown numbers were imprisoned or executed.

Originally published by *Chewers & Matiscadores*

9066 Soup

1.

Prof. Randy Burke walked into the library while texting with his mobile phone, "Which section are you in?"

"615"

"Will be there in a second."

Randy Burke climbed to the third floor by the stairs and walked to the bookshelves of Medicine and Health. Erick was leafing through a book that must have been published decades ago. Seeing Prof. Burke, he put the book back on the shelf before taking a look at the aisle number, so he would remember where to find the book again.

Erick was a graduate student emphasizing early English literature, but he read everything. He was given the nickname Detective Bloom because he solved all kinds of problems, from historical myths to computer secrets, from ancient geographic perspective to contemporary bioscience. Born in the digital era, Erick nonetheless loved antique things. He hung in the library all day, checking out all kinds of publications, from very tattered books to microfilms. Nothing failed to stimulate his interests. Erick believed that old objects contained much more information than what one could find from the Internet, and he was so infatuated with old stuff. The library security guard, Mr. Goldsmith, once said Erick spent more time in the library than he did. Many times Goldsmith had to kick Erick out when the library hours were over.

Prof. Burke and Erick walked toward the gate, they were having coffee at the outdoor stand. It was April, new leaves had covered all the tree branches, and people lay on grass under the tender April sun.

"I have a case for you." Prof. Burke took a sip of his coffee from the thermos he brought with him all the time so he could avoid the coffee store's disposable paper cups.

"Was seaweed a traditional Irish food?" He said putting down his thermos.

This question could be easy, it also could be quite complicated. But if it was easy, Prof. Burke would not have come to the library to pick up Erick for coffee.

"Have you tried your own research?" Erick asked Randy. Randy Burke was in his early forties, he taught information technology in the School of Natural Science, and got acquainted with Erick Bloom when he took one semester of information technology a couple of years ago. Usually students from the School of Humanities did not take any courses of technology, so he paid more attention to Erick, hoping he would not get left behind without technology training comparable to other students. Erick had done all right in his class anyway. With goals different from other students who planned to become engineers or programmers, Erick brought in a broader perspective of information technology and a variety of topics to the class, even though his classmates thought he was a freak.

"I did, but I couldn't find a conclusive answer. I know my relatives from Ireland don't eat much seaweed, but here in California, there are Irish restaurants providing dishes with seaweed and emphasizing it's Irish traditional food."

Erick's first response was that seaweed was easy to find along the west coast, and Ireland is an island country with very long seashores, seaweed must be quite available in Ireland, too. But why was this important?

Randy Burke took out his mobile phone and showed an image to Erick. It was a screenshot of a Limp Noodle Store's Twitter, which said, "Looking for a lost recipe of traditional Irish seaweed soup brought from Cork to California after WWII by Irish immigrants."

"I don't know why I want to pursue it," Randy shrugged, "perhaps if a thing was not part of their traditions but was claimed to be in certain places, there might be some story worth digging up."

"Like the stories about Thanksgiving."

"Right. But I hope it is not as ugly as the Thanksgiving lies."

After the coffee, they sat there a little bit longer to enjoy the changing light under the trees, then Prof. Burke left for class. Erick used his smart phone to check out information about Irish Americans in California.

Large numbers of Irish immigrants to the US could be dated back after the Great Famine in the late 1840s. They first landed in New York and Massachusetts, then in California. Currently, there are about two million people identifying themselves as Irish-Americans, and California has the largest population of Irish-Americans. Erick stood up and walked back to the library.

He found Miss Landry at the multimedia center. Betty Landry was the most senior librarian there; she had worked in the university library for forty years. Betty must be close to Erick's grandmother's age, but kept an attitude of being curious to everything. When Erick was called Detective Bloom, he knew he should thank Betty who always assisted him to find the materials he needed to solve his questions.

"Miss Landry, do you like to eat seaweed?"

Betty was testing the programs of a computer, the library just updated the software of their information system. She warmly smiled at Erick, "Yes, I do. What is your case today?"

"How do you cook it?"

"I don't cook seaweed. But whenever I dine in a Japanese restaurant, I will order food with a lot of seaweed, like sushi."

"Not in Irish restaurants?"

Betty thought for a little moment, and said, "Yeah, in Patrick O, they have a stew cooked with seaweed."

"Where is the best place to find materials about Irish Americans?"

"Archive Room. There are governmental archives of immigrants."

"Cool." Erick ran toward the elevator.

2.

In April, 1942, Tim Shimono joined the long journey of interment with tens of thousands of his fellow Japanese Americans. Tim was twenty-three years old, he had just graduated from the University of California and started working for the Connor Lab, a small institute of nutrition studies under the California State government and funded by public grants as well as the Connor family. Tim liked his work and his colleagues, the teamwork was an extension of his carefree campus life. But after the attack of Pearl Harbor, every Japanese American became suspected of espionage, and in no time, they were forced to leave their hometowns by the federal government.

Each person could only bring one suitcase, Tim had to think hard about what he could take with him. He packed some clothes, important documents and photos of his family, a pair of spare shoes, several pairs of socks, and a small bag of rice. Tim wished he could take several books, but his cousin Edward Shimino asked him to bring a violin for him. Edward had two children, he and his wife needed to prepare things for their children. Unable to bring more books, Tim grabbed a notepad and several pens, perhaps he would need to write something down in the future.

Before taking off, Tim's colleague Fiona rushed to his place to see him off. She brought a pack of dried kombu for Tim. Seeing how full his suitcase was, Tim was going to reject Fiona's gift, but Fiona tore open the pack and wrapped the dried kombu into her handkerchief. With reduced volume, they were able to squeeze it into Tim's suitcase. Seeing Tim walk off, Fiona withheld her agitation as long as she could, and burst into tears when Tim's profile disappeared at the street corner.

Fiona and Tim met in their work and several months ago as they started to work on a project together. It was a commission from the Society of Irish Americans, they hoped to root out the problems causing malnutrition in their community. The common occupations of Irish Americans in California were as small business owners, such as running eateries or pubs, hardware stores or groceries. Many of them worked as butlers for wealthy families, or builders of railroads and bridges like their ancestors a century ago. Women often were household helpers or nannies, those with better education became teachers or tutors. Most of them did not make great money, and had to live thriftily, especially those who had just settled in the US or had relatives just settled in the US. In order to save money, they probably were not eating enough to sustain their nutrition needs, and symptoms of malnutrition showed, like low stamina in teenagers, osteoporosis in women, and weak immunity in the elderly. So the Society wished to find affordable food and recipes with high nutrition values to recommend to their people. It was not a difficult task, but it takes time and professionalism to find the answers. Fiona was a descendant of Irish ancestry, she was given the mission to interview Irish families and find what food they usually bought, and how they cooked.

After several weeks of field investigation, Fiona realized that, from the perspective of a nutritionist, the people of her community needed more protein and vitamins, but it was what they couldn't afford. They couldn't afford to buy a lot of meat or seafood.

It was when Fiona and Tim started going out together after working together. It turned out to be a good thing for such an office romance, because after dining together several times and discussing their project, Tim said, "Japanese Americans are not rich, either, and the health issues of Irish Americans don't seem to be showing up among our Japanese population. Let's compare the diets of these two populations."

At first they did not see apparent differences between these two groups.

"Perhaps the scope of our samples is not big enough?" Fiona was worried. If they needed to investigate more families, they certainly would spend all the funds for this project before any constructive conclusion could be made.

"I don't think so." Tim looked at their notes again. In order to exclude bias, they visited the families of both communities together, in case their familiarity of their own culture would make them overlook significant affairs. The beautiful young couple were welcomed by people from both communities. But even though they were so careful, they still couldn't find any clue.

"Poor people go to the same markets and buy the same food." Tim said. He couldn't hide his frustration, but encouraged Fiona to put their work aside for a weekend, perhaps something would come up if they looked at it after a break.

3.

Detective Erick Bloom did not notice how late it was until Miss Betty Landry came to tell him the library was closing. It happened very often that Erick was driven out by Betty when the public hours were over.

The Archive Center was mixed with intriguing smells, mildewy, antique, something that was unrestorable… Were smells what intrigued Erick? Were they sensible? Unlike archived texts or graphs or charts, were smells transformed in time?

It was not the first time Erick got pushed out of

the library by Betty. Betty joked that Erick was the detective-in-residency of the library. Today, Betty offered to treat him to dinner at Patrick O. Erick, who suddenly realized he had only had breakfast and a cup of coffee with Prof. Burke all day, happily accepted and went with her.

Although Patrick O called itself Irish cuisine, its menu consists of hamburgers, French fries, tacos, even pastas. Erick found the kombu soup on the menu: 9066 Soup—Traditional Irish stew with skirts, potato and kombu. He asked the waiter why it was called 9066. The waiter, a college girl who shook her head, "Don't know, just started waiting on tables a week ago, and you are the first one inquiring about it." Thinking for a moment, she said, "You want me to ask my boss before making orders?

"I can order it first, and if you have time to inquire it for me…"

Betty ordered a piece of rhubarb tart and a cup of tea, and Erick scooped some of his soup to share with her.

"It's really delicious. I like the slimy texture from kombu." Erick praised, and Betty agreed. But no answer came up about why the soup was named 9066.

"Perhaps I can try to cook it at home." Betty said, "And you will be the first to taste my cooking."

"Where can you get the seaweed?"

Betty thought for a second, "Asian stores frequented by Japanese Americans?"

Erick's eyes wide opened, he grabbed Betty's hand, "Let's go! Let's go back to the library!"

"It's closed, can't we do it tomorrow?" Betty stood up, but protested.

"Please, I just realized I missed very important clues about this case in the Archive Center!"

"What?"

"This case, Prof. Burke's question about whether seaweed is traditional food for Irish people, and why this soup is called 9066!" Erick begged Betty, whom he knew would be curious enough to use her privilege to open the back door of the library for an emergency situation. It wasn't the first time anyway.

4.

Life in Camp Amache, Colorado was depressing, but the internees tried their best to elevate their living quality and mentality. They manufactured simple furniture, quilts, or wool socks for local people, but a lot of times they were still the hated Japs allied with the enemy that people did not want to deal with.

They established their own schools for children who had to drop out when they were forced into the internment camps. They found fellow internees qualified to be teachers of math, natural science, art, music and dance. Older people began to teach the Japanese language, and many adults joined their kids to learn it, too.

After several months of being relocated here, they were allowed to grow food at the empty sites of the camp. They grew peas, daikons, and potatoes. Tim suddenly remembered that he was given a pack of dried kombu by Fiona when he was leaving home. He took out the light green handkerchief buried at the bottom of his suitcase and carefully opened it. The dried kombu was still good, it smelled of home mixed with a slight whiff of Fiona's odour. Also in the handkerchief was a piece of the notepad they used for their project. Tim recalled that Fiona told him, "I was going to copy down the recipe, but I realized you are leaving now so I tore it down first. I will make it up later." It was a recipe they wrote together, a soup cooked with kombu and potatoes, to make up the stew of pork skirts and kidneys Irish people ate at home but might not be available in California. Kombu was rich with B vitamins along with other nutrients, such as calcium and iron, and even protein. With very affordable kombu, Irish people in California would make up the nutrition they needed in daily diets. They came up with this idea through a trip to the Bay Area on a weekend. On the beach they saw several Japanese people collect seaweed between the rocks after the tides faded away. It was the major difference of the diets between Japanese Americans and Irish Americans around this area.

Tim shared the dried kombu Fiona gave him with others, they cooked soup with the vegetables they had harvested from their gardens. Without much meat, kombu provided rich flavors and nutritional value comparable to meat. Later when postal service began to be served to the internees, they began to receive dried kombu from their friends in California. It greatly made up for the depressing life in the camp.

Without knowing what would be his fate, Tim had decided not to contact Fiona anymore when he left home, even though Fiona bade him many many times that once he settled somewhere, he must write to her. Looking at the address Fiona wrote down for him so carefully and so determinedly, Tim thought, I should write her a letter.

5.

In the Archive room, they lit only lights above the shelves that Erick had gone through earlier, in case they got busted by Mr. Goldsmith. He quickly pulled out drawers one by one to find objects he had seen but did not pay much attention. Finally in a cardboard box, he found a notepad belonging to a nutrition lab almost eighty years ago. Erick flipped it to a torn page. From the remaining text, it was a recipe, and from the text of other pages, it was a report on the diets of Irish descendants in California, and the recipe was one of the suggestions of the investigators.

"This is the recipe for the soup we just had!"

"How do you know?" Betty asked.

Erick showed Betty the names of the researchers, Tim Shimoto and Fiona Qinn, "Tim Shimono was a Japanese American, and the Executive Order 9066 was the order President Roosevelt signed to force Japanese Americans from the west coast to move to the camps in the inner land."

"Before Tim Shimono was relocated, he tore down the recipe and brought it with him?" Betty speculated.

"I think so. The recipe was for Irish people to cook low cost meals, Shimino must think he might need it in difficult situations."

"And after the war, it became an invented tradition among Irish food suppliers."

"Yes. It explains Prof. Burke's doubt, why Irish in Ireland don't think seaweed is their traditional food, but Irish in California do. It was not from Cork, it was made up here."

"It is a legacy from eighty years ago. There is a bad side and then there is a good side." Betty concluded.

Erick and Betty put out the lights and silently closed the library door again. They imagined the life of Tim Shimino during the war and after the war, and recollected the delicious soup they just had together.

Originally published by *The Short Story Town*

Pronunciation Practice

1.

He sank in the water, letting the flow bring him down. It felt so good, the coldness in the stream. He thought of lifting his head to get air, but the water was so tender, so caring, he decided to stop breathing and bury himself further into the stream, leaving his troubles behind.

A moment ago, Redage was ordered by his classmates to kneel down and apologize to them for nothing he had done. Redage refused, so they threw rocks at him, kicked his knees. They kicked him so forcefully in order to injure his joints, so he would conform, or, too hurt to stand up.

It was not the first time. He had been bullied by these boys since he enrolled in this school, a school he thought he could learn gymnastics. Redage performed well in school, but he couldn't get along with his classmates, or, to be correct, they couldn't get along with him. Redage's dark skin was mocked, and his insufficient vocabulary of Mandarin was criticized.

"Hey, you indigenous boy, you are more like an animal than a human. That's the reason why you jump higher."

"Redage, you speak like an idiot. Are you an idiot?"

"My sandwich disappeared. Redage, you stole my lunch, right? I know it was you, don't deny it, I have witnesses." Redage did not even know what a sandwich was. He never stole anything, he did not have to.

Redage was hardly left alone, he was hassled when he was eating, sleeping, and studying. It was an experience he never had when he was in his hometown. In his tribal community, Redage was well taken care of not only by his parents and his siblings, but also everyone in the village. He was a jewel in the eye of his people, and when he was admitted by the school in the city, they congratulated him by killing a boar to share with the entire clan. They wished him a bright career as a professional athlete, to clean the name of his tribal people as barbarians. "Bully" was a new thing to Redage, he never knew people from a different world could be so mean. Who were more uncivilized?

Redage's right knee was hurt so much by the

relentless attacks of his classmates. But he couldn't surrender. The pride that was his birthright did not allow him to beg for mercy from these villains. He jumped into the creek. He was not running away, he was seeking relief from the things he was familiar with. The creek water, the soul sustaining medium, he was a part of it.

2.

It's eight o'clock at night, I must finish my homework before that, and start my pronunciation practice. It's an agenda my mother set, she wants us to speak perfect Mandarin. At first she would pick up one piece of reading material for me and my two sisters, each of us read it with the best Mandarin pronunciation we could manage, then we took turns correcting one another.

We are from the Rukai Tribe. My mother left her community to work as a missionary when she was eighteen years old. She was recruited by the pastor from the Presbyterian church in their village to be trained as a missionary in the city. Mom worked several years as an assistant to several missionaries after the training, and decided to stay and work in the city.

Mom's first job was in the kitchen of an elementary school. It was the beginning when she first began to understand what discrimination was. Mom's co-workers decided she was the lowest among the kitchen staff because she was from the remote mountain area, belonging to the "world of savages". Mom was assigned to do the jobs the others did not want, cleaning the restrooms, taking trash out, and mopping the floor. One time the director of discipline of the school came to check the kitchen work before the visit of the supervisors from the bureau of education, he murmured something to the head of the kitchen staff. The next day Mom was forbidden from touching any food.

Because of my dark skin, I must be dirty?

Later Mom changed several jobs and with the little wages she earned she finished her college degree. She had been working in the warehouse of a supermarket, a gas station, and a Hong Kong food restaurant. Once Mom was advised to work as a betel nut girl, wearing very sexy outfits in the booths by highways. She was told she could make much more money if she could attract as many long-distance truck drivers as possible who need to chew betel nuts to stay awake. But Mom was clear that if she wanted to have a career instead of a better income, she needed to choose an industry or a profession.

Mom became an excellent architecture model

maker. She first worked for an architect, and built models with several designers, most of them were men. Mom's ability to read architectural diagrams impressed them, they let her prepare the materials, such as paper boards, plastic panels, styrofoams, tooth picks, and a variety of glues. Mom was also quite good in estimating the quantities of each material for a model, her skill saved a lot of expense for the architecture firm.

Mom was happy with her work as a professional architecture model maker, her salary was satisfying, and she got along with her colleagues. But she hardly shared her background with her colleagues, she did not want them to know that she was an indigenous woman from a "savage village" in the mountains. Since my teenage years, I noticed Mom always chose facial creams emphasizing the function of "whitening". I guessed it worked, because Mom's skin was indeed quite fair, compared to mine.

I was born a dark baby, and my skin tone was a worry for Mom. I believe she must have applied her whitening cream, probably a more expensive brand, over me when I was little, but obviously it did not work well. My father has dark skin, too, but I am not sure if it's from sun tan or genes. Dad is half indigenous, half Han.

Worrying that I will be treated unfairly, my

mother insists that we all must speak perfect Mandarin. I am not against perfecting my Mandarin, in fact, raised and educated in the city, I have no problem in speaking perfect Mandarin at all. So the pronunciation practice every night is more for me to correct my parents' speaking and grammar, and my reading of articles my mother selected for us from the newspapers.

"Kneecap, bracket, patella, bracket… is it Hsi Gai, or Chu Gai?" Dad asked, not sure how to pronounce "knee" in Mandarin.

"Hsi, Hsi Gai. I've corrected you so many times already. It's not Chu. 'Chu' makes the knee bend, but your knees don't have to bend, OK?"

"Alright, alright. Hsi Gai, not Chu Gai…" Dad carefully wrote down the phonetic symbols next to the characters that confused him so many times."

"Dad, it's easy to remember it with a C, like the C from A, B, C." My younger sister said.

"Oh, that's right!" Dad put a large C on his notepad, "With this I won't forget it again. C, from A, B, C." He smiled satisfactorily.

Mom seems to be lost in the train of her thoughts. Sometimes I can't help but think Mom's ideas of assimilating us into the mainstream are ridiculous. Why can't we see ourselves from our own perspective but from that of the mainstream?

3.

When Redage's body was found, his skin was so pale after soaking in the water for hours. His sister Vauvauni couldn't recognize him, or, she refused to believe it was her baby brother's body. She noticed his right knee was injured badly, and a large area of his muscles showed bruises. She wanted to touch it, to relieve the pain he must have suffered, but she couldn't. Redage looked so fragile, it seemed that he would fall apart if she touched him.

The official story from Redage's school was that he fell into the water while playing with his classmates and drowned in the fast currents. But Redage was such a good swimmer, he could swim in waters much more dire than the stream he was found in.

Looking back, Vauvauni had to admit that Redage had lost his smile since he started going to the school in town. Stories about how hard it was for indigenous peoples to live in the cities began to be passed on to their family. Perhaps they knew it all the time, just they chose not to believe it, not to face it. After all, it was Redage's dream to be a professional gymnast.

Teenage boys needed to find victims for their evil egos, and a person with a different appearance was a perfect target. Redage's unusual talents in sports became his burden. If he did his best in his performance, he'd be given a hard time. His classmates reported him to the teachers with the most trivial matters, like if he did not bring his handkerchief, or if he left the door of the gear room unlocked. Redage might be tripped by one of them unexpectedly when he was running, or he might find his bag dampened by dirty water. He began to realize that staying down by performing mediocre was the best way to avoid conflicts, but he was in despair not able to learn much in classes.

Vauvauni never could forgive herself. Had she inquired Redage what had really happened to him in school, they might decide it was better to take him home. But the whole family's belief that Redage certainly would become a super star in sports blinded them, they did not suspect the danger in Redage's school life.

The wounded knee. For a long time Vauvauni couldn't remember how her little brother looked when he was alive. The only image of Redage imprinted in her head since his death was his wounded right knee. Redage's wounded knee, her older sister's nightmare for years.

4.

My mom always vaguely suggests that I should avoid exposing myself under sunlight too much.

She advises me to use sunblock, an umbrella, and facial cream that will "brighten" my skin tone. I always laugh off my mother's ideas, which are so unnecessary and impossible. I am such a good athlete, I participate in my school's games and training as often as possible, track running, high jump, long jump and swimming. There is simply no way I can avoid sunlight. One of my strengths in sports is that I perform better than other girls in scorching heat. My indigenous identity is rightly respected, although not really understood. I once volunteered to teach my teammates how to swim fast in a river, but our self-training program shocked our coach and teachers who immediately forbad us from doing it again. They thought it was too dangerous for anyone to swim in fast currents. We had fun, though. And I believe my teammates have improved their swimming skills.

I also like to try gymnastics, but my school has no instruments or instructors for gymnastics. I mentioned it when we were in my mother's tribal community, and it was the first time I heard about my uncle, who died about the age I am now.

Every summer my parents will take us back to their hometown, it is the most important thing to us each year. Their hometown is in the remotest mountain in southern Taiwan, each year we will have to drag our luggage and presents we prepare for our relatives in the mountains and take bus to the train station, and after a long train trip, we still need to take two bus rides to the village at the foothill of my parents' mountain. At there we either call our relatives to pick us up, or hitchhike to my mother or my father's community. Vehicles taking us and our big luggage usually are trucks, on the bumpy and winding road we are tired but happy since it means we are close to our destination. For the trip to my parents' hometown, we usually take off as early as dawn, and arrive as late as midnight.

When all my classmates are in the summer camps of backpacking, English learning, creative writing, or basketball playing… I am in the remote mountains, reviewing my parents' mother tongue with elders and my cousins, and swimming in the streams that my ancestors called "roads walked by fishes". The streams nourish us, they are abundant and giving; we belong to them.

It is also the time my Mandarin is laughed at.

"You speak like a Beijinger."

On the plain, it is a compliment because people in Taiwan believe that the down-to-earth Mandarin came from Beijing, and speaking like a Beijinger is the goal for people like anchormen and anchor-women from TV news channels. But in the tribal community, a girl with dark skin and curly hair like me is not expected to speak like a Beijinger. Behind my mother, I'd mimick the accent of my cousins. To my ears, they speak Mandarin like singing. In fact, they communicate with one another by singing very often. Many social codes are contained in the singing, but I can't distinguish them.

One night we all sat in the open space in the center of the community, under a Large-Leaved Nanmu tree. I was asked how I was doing in school. I never bothered to tell them how good I was in math, science, or Chinese classics, I knew they were not really interested. So I told them what sports I was exercising and racing. I told them I wish I could learn gymnastics.

"You know who could be an excellent gymnast? Redage!" Granduncle Sula said; he was close to being drunk. All others fell into silence.

Embarrassed, Sula's wife stood up and walked toward him, "Didn't you say you are checking the boar trap you set this afternoon?" She pulled Sula from his seat, and they walked away together.

The others remained silent for a while longer, then they began talking about something else.

I still don't know much about Redage, who I believe was my uncle, my mother's younger brother she never mentioned to us. I also vaguely understand why my mom cares so much about my accent, my skin tone, and how I am getting along with my peers. It is not because of her vanity or illusion that being like the others will make our social status higher than our true indigenous identities, but being who we are could be shameful, undignified, and even tragic.

5.

I bury my face in the water. Rocks on the riverbed remind me of the huge mountains surrounding our community, their colors shine in sunlight, grey like my grandpa's hair, brown like my uncle's skin, green like my mother's leek. I am always in awe looking up at them under the holy sky. No view can be broader than what I am seeing at this moment. Now they are surrounding me again.

The cool water flows past my hair, my shoulders, my stretched arms, my back and chest, my waist, my hips, my thighs, my knees, and my feet. It heals my wounded knee. It is sacred, I am purified and delivered. I am not going back to the world above water. I am melting into it, I am lifted when I reach the deepest. I am a part of it. I am.

Originally published by *Hennepin Review*

Over the Other Side of the Road

Over the other side of the road, beyond the poorly maintained paths winding through your tribal community, lies a different world.

Choosing a name with two syllables like Hsiu-Mei, Ming-Jun, or Lin-Yun instead of Rimuy, Selep, Ival, Wagi, or Faizu, which people struggle to pronounce and mistakenly associate you with an immigrant from the unknown south.

Using whitening facial cream bought from a cosmetic store near a subway station, promising fairer skin after two weeks of daily use, so you can blend in with any other office lady in modern society.

Practicing your proficiency in the official language, ensuring that your mountain accent goes unnoticed by others.

Leaving behind the tales passed down by your ancestors and embracing the rock & roll music favored by other youth. Abandoning the knowledge of forests and rivers taught by your elders and adapting to the lifestyle in an urban jungle.

Forgetting about the grilled meat of boars or Reeve's muntjac, soup made from wild mushrooms, stir-fried nest fern, and steamed quinoa, as well as the millet wine and energy drink mixed with fermented grains. Opting for sandwiches, bentos, rice, or noodles processed in industrial kitchens instead of over stone fire rings.

Over the other side of the road, beyond the poorly maintained paths winding through your tribal community, lies a different world.

Assuming an identity other than your true self, so you can avoid confronting the complex issues that make it difficult and miserable to be yourself, because over the other side of the road, it is a different world to your tribal community.

A Collector of Indigenous Songs

He visits our tribal community and elaborately writes down what he hears during our worship of ancestors. And we sing *lmuhuw* in memory of their decisions of finding new places for our growing tribe.

> 'uwrqes na 'llaqiy qani, hala sami patupucing
> innwahan lyus na 'lawy mamu, ru hala sami mtatusa, uw atu na agiq ma qu wah.

"Children, go, we follow traces of walking, knife cuts, you and our sprawling grass."

ta is "we", *sami* is "our"?

He gets completely perplexed with the changing subjects, reversed sentence structures and metaphors.

atu na agiq, sprawling grass?

It means offspring, sir.

He signs. He gets different answers for the same question from different people, and each day he gets different explanations of the same term.

That's why we don't write them down, sir.

Our languages are passed down by mouth and ears, not by pens.

Originally published by *New Feathers Anthology*

A Bystander of His Hometown

Domas is an indigenous Atayal writer, he has a Han name Lee Yung-Sung. Domas's mother was Atayal, his father was half Han and half Atayal. Domas's grandfather was working as a camphor collector during the Japanese colonial era. At that time, Taiwan produced 70% of the world's camphor. But of course, it was deemed as a "Japanese product". Domas's grandfather Yumin worked in the watershed of the Dakekan Creek, the traditional territory of Atayal people. Roughly processed camphor would be shipped to Taipei through waterways, and in Taipei it was processed again into final products before being exported. Camphor collecting was a highly professional job, collectors had to be able to distinguish seven different species of camphor trees by their smell. Camphor collectors in Taiwan were making great wages and were exempted from being drafted to fight WWII in Southeast Asia for the Japanese Imperial Army.

Yumin married Lawa and settled down in the indigenous Qehuy community; they had four children, and Domas's father Kagi was one of them. Kagi's wife, Domas's mother Amui also was a local girl. From Amui, Domas and his brother inherited 17 hectares of land by the Dakekan Creek. To people from the city, it was an extremely valuable waterfront location with a splendid view.

Most of the uncleared lands in the Qehuy area were bamboo forests on slopes facing the creek. Decades ago, bamboo grown and cut here was procured by Han people at very low prices as building material or for furniture. For indigenous peoples, inheritance meant being given the right to make use of those things the land provided, at the same time they were obliged to maintain those things the lands provided without abusing it. In Domas's case, he grew yam leaves, pears, nectarines and other vegetables or fruits. He also harvested wild bamboo sprouts in Spring. Unfortunately, throughout Domas's adulthood, he had witnessed the land owners around his property selling their lands for the development of resorts, campgrounds or amusement parks.

Since these lands were traditional indigenous territory, how could they be sold? In fact, it was a form of manipulation in which the land owners borrowed money using their properties as collateral, so their creditors had the right to clear the lands and build things on them. There were no laws against such manipulation, and thus gradually indigenous territories throughout Taiwan were exploited, including what were supposed to be source water protection zones or other ecologically sensitive areas.

Domas's land was the only lot that was still untouched by developers, and he had to say no to interested developers every now and then. His neighbors thought Domas was crazy, as a writer without much income, his persistence to possess a land yielding nothing but a meager, worthless crop was but the proof of Domas's insanity.

Each day Domas went to his land to take care of his fruit trees, flowers, and vegetables. Little by little, he also repaired the deteriorating trails that his ancestors walked during their camphor collecting. At night he wrote his novel and did research about ancestral assets he was slowly losing—the Atayal culture and language. Before going to bed, he climbed to his roof to drink by himself. Surrounded by the brightly lit campground, the fancy camping gears on the concrete floors, and the expensive SUVs parking along the roads paved over antique camphor trails, Domas felt he was a solo bystander of his deformed hometown.

Originally published by *Out West Writings*

Millions of Ants

Just a few years ago, it was unimaginable that martyrdom for democracy could pertain to either one of us, or even both of us. But now, I am consumed with frustration and unable to focus on my daily routines. My daughter, Kasia, had finally been released from prison, and I had hoped that her return would bring peace to our lives. However, her presence at home was bothered by our own uncertainty and detachment.

Most days, Kasia retreated to her bedroom and remained quiet. I was left to wonder what she was doing inside, afraid that she had become disconnected from the outside world or, worse yet, that she had become entrenched in the world that had led to her imprisonment. And where did I, her mother, fit into all of this? I had once been proud of her activism and involvement in public affairs. When Kasia was just fifteen, she bravely protested the nationalistic and moralistic curriculum being imposed on

Hong Kong's elementary and high schools. To us, this curriculum was nothing more than brainwashing that served no purpose in Hong Kong. Eventually, the curriculum was withdrawn after students' rigorous protests. However, over the past few years, the Education Bureau had implemented various curricular schemes without any public input. These courses emphasized official Chinese history and outdated themes of family values packaged as civic affairs lessons. I couldn't help but wonder why the Bureau failed to prioritize human rights. While they included topics regarding cultural identity, history, and civic affairs, they neglected to address fundamental issues of human dignity and freedom.

Anyway, the withdrawal of the brainwashing curriculum gave Kasia and her peers great confidence, they felt they could accomplish anything. I was also optimistic, I supported Kasia's active participation in public affairs, and encouraged her to debate on issues that mattered.

But now, I can't help but wonder if my optimism was misplaced. Did I put Kasia in harm's way? Was I to blame for her imprisonment and her current unease?

We must be too naive when we teach our young people to speak up for justice or defend freedom, not only for ours, but also for that of others. It was the mentality of an open society that had already attained freedom, like the US, Europe, Japan, South Korea and Taiwan. All these societies had been through a long and bitter journey to earn their freedom, but for those of us in Hong Kong, our long fight has just begun.

It is easy to fall into the illusion that victory is assured when we look at the successful examples from history textbooks, biographies of historical figures, or political analyses by historians. We may believe that constant protests, united with those who share our beliefs, will ultimately lead to triumph. We romanticized past revolutions because the martyrs and survivors who fought for change are long gone from our time, and we do not bear witness to the immense sacrifices and struggles they had endured.

It can take a confined society decades of fighting to achieve liberation, yet a free society can fall into the hands of dictatorship overnight. We never could have imagined that one day we had to debate on whether carrying a flag with words such as "liberation" and "revolution" is an act of terrorism or secession. Can a person terrorize the society or secede from the country by simply tying a flag to their scooter?

If the government were not corrupt, if policy-making were transparent, and if politicians could take in different ideas or listen to criticism without abusing their authority, who would feel the needs to demonstrate in the rain or under the scorching sun to express their discontent or disappointment? Fighting for one's rights is not terrorism, it is not secession. Yet today, any remark or action expressing one's disagreement with the public affairs could be labeled as such, and the responses of the authorities to dissident opinions were definitely more terrifying.

One night a couple of years ago, when Kasia and her friend Anthony were walking home together after a group meeting, they were ambushed by three men in a small alleyway. The assailants pinned Anthony against the wall, one of them elbowing him in the eyes while the other two held him down by his neck, hands, and legs, making it impossible for him to fight back. Kasia screamed at the top of her lungs and tried to pull the attackers away from Anthony, but one of the men kicked her in the calf and then again in the head while she was bent over in pain.

They shouted:

"You're organizing a student strike, aren't you?" they sneered at Anthony before delivering another punch to his face.

"Well, we're warning you to back off. If you don't, next time we meet, you won't leave with your limbs intact." The attackers then turned their attention to Kasia, giving her a nasty look,

"And as for your little girlfriend, well... you know what we mean," they taunted with a lewd grin before finally departing.

Anthony had to stay in hospital for a whole week, his eyes swelled so badly that they were afraid he might lose his eyesight permanently. Fortunately his eyes recovered, but the injury on the back of his head left him with recurring bad headaches that seemed incurable. Anthony, Kasia and their fellow activists never talked about strikes again.

They had a plan to hold a voting with no fewer than ten thousand students, and if more than 60% of voters voted for strike, they would advocate for an island-wide student strike as part of their movement. But their actions were disturbed by school administrations, concerned parents, as well as attacks or threats like the ones Anthony and Kasia had encountered.

Anthony never talked about that night with Kasia. Did Kasia feel guilty about Anthony's attack? Could she help it under such circumstances? What if... What if they had hurt Kasia, too? I couldn't bring myself to think about it any longer.

Now all the groups for social movements, including their Demosisto, disbanded after the implementation of the National Security Law. From news reports in Taiwan, I learned that Anthony moved to the UK after hiding in Taiwan for almost one year. In Hong Kong, he was stalked and watched all the time, and he couldn't fall asleep until dawn. The fear his attackers had implanted in his mind had completely taken away his freedom.

And what had happened during Kasia's imprisonment? Was she violated in any form? Should I inquire with her directly? Should I seek help from experts? Were Kasia and Anthony still in touch? What kinds of things would they exchange if they were? Should I exhaust all available means to send Kasia to the UK, too? However, Kasia had renounced her UK citizenship in 2018, when she decided to run for the office of the Legislative Council. Later her candidacy was disqualified, with the excuse that her campaign for Hong Kong's self-determination was the proof of her negligence of the Basic Law. Why can't I protect my girl at home and have to send her away? How is Anthony's mother? How did she cope with her son being tortured so much and finally running away? How is Anthony now? Is he sleeping well now? What kind of people are around him in the UK? Does he feel safe? Anthony is only 23 years old, and Kasia is only 26. What I was doing when I was their age? It was in the early 1990s, I went to college, took a part-time job in a gallery and later worked as a research project assistant for my professor. My dream was to save some money and travel to Europe, to take the train across Europe—the sort of travel that had fascinated me in novels and movies.

When I was Kasia's age now, I was in love with her father. We dated, we took walks in the bustling city, ate street food, and watched Hollywood movies in the cinema. We met up in the college library and thought we could study together but we fooled around all the time. We were almost care-free, the only thing we worried about was that we did not save enough money to travel to Europe. Kasia worked with many boys during her activism, and they were all great people, they had ideals, they took care of one another. But obviously with so many risks in their lives, it was not time for them to develop any romantic relationship. Would Kasia be in love one day, even as so many of her fellow activists were either in prisons or overseas?

Kasia was born in the summer of 1997, the year of Hong Kong's handover from the UK to China. Hong Kong was guaranteed that its political system would remain unchanged for 50 years. Naturally it was assumed that in fifty years, China would be an open society, a freer place. The promise was not kept, instead, propaganda began after fewer than twenty years, followed by tightening control. Could we foresee its coming? Did we miss any chance to prevent it?

"Kasia, do you want to take Cornbread back?" I asked when Kasia came to the kitchen to take the food I prepared for her. Cornbread was the cat she got from Daniel, before he left Hong Kong and went to Boston for graduate school. Kasia loved Cornbread so much, and I think her love of Cornbread was also a reflection of her friendship and comradeship with Daniel and Daniel's gay lover Ben. Ben was still in prison. He was sentenced to eighteen months incarceration for "inciting unapproved political gatherings", the same charge resulting in Kasia's imprisonment. Right after Kasia's imprisonment, I took Cornbread to my cousin Marie, because Cornbread showed extreme anxiety staying in a home without Kasia.

Kasia thought for a moment and said, "No." She did not explain why she denied my suggestion. Cornbread would be happy to unite with Kasia, why did Kasia not want to take Cornbread back? She adored the kitty so much. Wouldn't cuddling with Cornbread in bed bring Kasia comfort on sleepless nights? I did not know how to pursue it, instead, I inquired carefully before Kasia returned to her bedroom:

"Should we mail Ben something he might need

in...?" I still couldn't speak out the word "prison".

"Probably not, I was told that Ben will be released on bail soon. But we can mail some sanitary pads to my former cellmates." Kasia said. Female prisoners in the prison where Kasia was incarcerated were not given enough sanitary pads, their families had to mail them. After Kasia's release, I realized Kasia's menstruation during her incarceration had become irregular first, then completely stopped. Whenever she got sanitary pads I mailed her, she gave them to her cellmates.

Was her period normal now? Should I ask? Kasia ate less than she used to, she had lost some weight. I would think losing appetite and having a sleep disorder might affect her menstrual cycle.

Perhaps Ben would want Cornbread back after he was freed. Would Cornbread understand what had been going on and why she was sent away so many times? In chaotic times, even a kitty can not be left in peace. I had seen a photo of Daniel holding Cornbread, he smiled happily, like a little child. They were all so young and so innocent, and now they all became political prisoners or exiled. Daniel was awarded a full scholarship from Harvard, it was a kind of rescue from the university.

Those who left Hong Kong and found asylum in other countries, such as Taiwan, the US or the

UK, often felt guilty for not staying in Hong Kong to continue their fight. They didn't think they deserved the right to be free when their fellow activists were still confined. They were worried that their efforts outside of Hong Kong wouldn't change much of Hong Kong's situation, just like Anthony told the reporter from Taiwan that after the Tiananmen Massacre, the exiled dissidents failed to change the Chinese regime.

Is it possible at all to overturn an authoritarian regime? For millions of Hong Kongers, their simple wish to have basic rights had not even been allowed. In the anti-extradition parades in June, 2019, two million people took the streets to express their objections. Why couldn't the will of millions of people change anything? To an authoritarian regime, people were nothing but ants. Authoritarians didn't give the slightest concern for humanity. To the authorities, millions of people were no more than millions of ants, they could be stomped to death without any empathy.

"Are you watching it, Kasia?" One afternoon I came back from grocery shopping and saw the TV was on. It was very unusual that Kasia was watching something on the TV in our living room these days, she always watched videos on her laptop in her bedroom.

"Yeah. I want to see how to cut hair myself. My laptop is too small to check out the details."

"Oh? You want to cut your hair?"

Kasia had grown her hair long since she was a little girl.

"Yeah, so people won't recognize me so easily."

Did this mean Kasia was going out of our apartment? Should I have felt happy for her or worried about her? Kasia had become a known person since the Umbrella Movement, she was called Umbrella Princess. I never liked this nickname. The day of Kasia's release, these two words appeared in the news media again. I hoped those who were obsessed with heroism or fairy tales would leave Kasia alone. After all, revolution couldn't be achieved by any princess.

Now we have all learned about the cruelty of political movements under a dictator, and Kasia's princess look did not help her at all. I envisaged Kasia had her hair cut short, she changed into a completely different person, unimpressed and characterless. Then she walked into the multitude and became unseen.

In today's Hong Kong, if any change was possible at all, it would be achieved by millions of ants.

Originally published by *Leo Literary Magazine*

It Took Us 50 Years

"It's a substantial amount of money, Sis. Aren't you worried that they might spend it recklessly?"

"Why should I be worried? These young people could be arrested and put in jail anytime, just like our ancestors. I couldn't care less how they spend my money."

Florence was speaking to her younger sister in Taiwan on the phone, and both of them knew they should not talk too much about this topic. They changed the topic to the music they had been working on recently.

Lately Florence had been reselling her designer accessories to a consignment store: a white Saint Laurent shoulder bag she had picked out for herself for her 15th wedding anniversary, a steel blue Chloé calfskin handbag she had bought in Milan, a Burberry wool cape she had only worn once, a dark red Salvatore Ferragamo belt given to her by Lisa when she left their common agent, and a pair of navy blue

Stella McCartney boots that she had worn for the ceremony of the Golden Melody Awards. Florence also had many hats and scarves she had bought while traveling, and she would resell some of them, the more expensive ones.

Florence hoped these hardly-used high-end products could be sold at a discount of 30% to 50% of their original prices, and in cash. Recently her income from the royalties of her albums had drained up due to the cheap sharing streams and the fast tides of young singers of newer music styles. Florence's career was in the popular music industry, and at the peak of it, she had lived like a superstar in Taiwan and Hong Kong. She was also well-known in China and Singapore, along with other Chinese speaking societies. Like many stars married to rich businessmen, Florence was proposed to by a successful Hong Kong businessman, Simon Liu, during the most rewarding time of her career. For the first years of her marriage, Florence had flown between Taipei and Hong Kong to maintain her career, but soon her husband's family expressed their displeasure about her being a singer. Wasn't it ironic? Florence asked her sister Lily, "Didn't Simon propose to me because I was a very successful singer?

The snobbishness of the Liu Family estranged Florence from her husband, whose business involved real estate, securities, horse racing, and a lot of things that Florence wasn't interested in knowing about. But when Simon's mother was dying of cancer, Florence was her primary caretaker. Not that Florence took her filial duty seriously, especially in a family becoming more and more sadistic due to its overwhelming wealth, but because she was the only one who could handle the ill woman's declining body and soul with admirable calm. Florence's emotionally detached contribution drew praise from the relatives and friends of the Liu family, and she earned herself an HSBC gold credit card from Simon. That was how she had so many luxurious outfits and accessories, although the public occasions she attended were fewer and fewer as time went by. One time Florence brought Lily a Dior dress during a trip to her hometown in the remote area of Alishan mountain, but Lily just laughed out loud and said, "Sis, why do I need a dress like this? To greet hunters coming home from the hunt?"

"Sell it online, then." Florence laughed along with her.

They auctioned the dress online and donated the money to a band of teenagers from their community. After that initial donation, that was how Florence sponsored music events in her hometown. Florence never had much cash to spend. When she needed money, she bought things with her gold credit card and then resold them at a discount in order to obtain cash. From the bank bills, her husband could only see that she bought purses, outfits, shoes and other accessories of big brands from time to time. He couldn't know what she actually possessed. In their extravagant condominium in Hong Kong, Florence had a walk-in wardrobe to keep all the gifts she decided to give herself from her husband's money. That wardrobe was also the source of opportunities that she could generate for music talents in her small hometown.

Florence's tribal name was Akuan, and Lily's was Usu, and they belonged to the Tsou ethnicity. Since 2014, Florence had been donating the money she laundered through her accessories, one by one, to the young activists demanding direct elections in Hong Kong and against extraditing Hong Kong offenders to China. She brought cash to her contacts at certain times and certain places. In this way she left no trace at all. Lily knew what her sister was doing, although they did not talk about it much in case they were under surveillance. When Florence's donation for her hometown shrank because she was donating an equal amount of money to the democratic movements in Hong Kong, Lily would try her best to make it up, so the young people in their community who dreamed of a music career would not find their dreams interrupted.

Simon would not agree with Florence's support of the democracy activists, Florence knew that without having to talk to Simon about it. He was a businessman enjoying the success he had generated through the dense upper-class social network that his ancestors had built up over succeeding generations. Simon Liu was a typical person of vested interest; he would never see the true lives of Hong Kong people nor the true value of social equality. In the depth of her heart, Florence knew her family history connecting her to the victims of Taiwan's White Terror would eventually drive her to a course of life that was completely oblivious to Simon. But at this stage, Florence felt justified in extracting a little money from his tremendous wealth for the social movements.

On a Tuesday afternoon, the consignment store Fashionfeel near the Kimberly Plaza called Florence, telling her that her brand new azure Hermes lambskin gloves had sold. Florence called her contact to meet her in a food store nearby. Florence went to pick up her money first, then went to buy a box of sushi. As she was browsing in the supermarket, a young woman fitting the description of her contact, a pair of dark green mary jane shoes with a flowery buckle on each side, was buying a magazine. So Florence quickly handed the envelope of her money to the young woman.

As Florence walked out of the store, she immediately noticed that she was being followed. Florence walked into a bookstore, determined to spend at least a couple of hours reading as many books as possible. She hoped her stalker liked reading, too.

"She is under surveillance. Don't send her for such tasks any more," Florence told her contact on the phone soon after.

"Are you sure? How can you know?"

"Because right after we met, I was followed."

"Are you sure?"

"Believe me, I've been under surveillance since before you were born. Or more accurately, I've been under surveillance since before I was born."

***

In addition to all the legacies of her tribal culture, such as farming, hunting, building, wine making and dream interpretation, Florence also inherited the fears of her parents and grandparents from the White Terror period. Nothing is more frightening than something that has never been talked about. When Florence was a little girl, her grandpa was often away from home, and she vaguely knew that he was often summoned to the police station several miles from their community. In the mountains, walking was the only method of traveling, and the trip to the police station took grandpa a whole day. He had to put aside all his jobs to go, and he usually did not know when he would be called so he couldn't arrange his schedule in advance. Usually it was the village chief who got the phone call and ran to their home to notify Grandpa. It could be during the early morning, or around noon, or at nightfall, any time of any day. It could be when grandpa was working in the field, or having his meal, or in the middle of the family chores. There was no excuse for not going, and no delay was allowed.

Each time when Grandpa was gone, Grandma would be extremely anxious. What if he never returned, like his brother? Although Florence's parents would comfort Grandma that it would be all right and Grandpa would be home soon, Florence could feel that they were worried, too. Florence had overheard her parents secretly complaining about their uncle, who died twenty years before Florence's birth, for acting recklessly and causing trouble for all of them for such a long time. Nevertheless, they were also clear in their minds that no matter how obedient one was, people with unrestrained power would certainly abuse it.

Florence's granduncle 'Uongu was executed because he was "attempting to overturn the government by unlawful means." It was an early spring morning, according to Florence's grandparents, when they got a call from Taipei. A friend told them that their brother 'Uongu had been executed. It was one year and two months after his arrest, and they never had been told anything about his trial. They heard that all the names of the executed from the previous day would be listed on a board near the Taipei Railway Station, so they asked a relative working in a construction site around the area to check the names for them every morning. If he saw 'Uongu's name on it, he should make a phone call to their village. It was the first phone call they ever received in the village chief's place, on a morning at the end of winter in 1952.

Five decades later, when the national archives finally opened up for the victims, their families and researchers of the White Terror to look through, they knew 'Uongu's attempt to overturn the government was nothing but launching a group that urged for political reform and more direct participation in public affairs for indigenous peoples. So what was his unlawful means? At that time, in the name of national security, criticizing the regime was unlawful.

And the death of 'Uongu was just the beginning of their nightmare. After the very simple burial of 'Uongu, they realized they were under extremely strict surveillance. 'Uongu's brother, Yaipuku, who naturally had knowledge about his brother's political standing, was deemed as the number one suspect as his brother's accomplice and became the subject of close investigation. According to the logic of the regime at that time, all the people in their community were possible national traitors. So their freedom should be restricted in order to prevent their probable actions against the nation again, or as punishment for being the family of a convicted national traitor. The "investigation" lasted for decades. Even children born many years after 'Uongu's death were suspected of treason. Gradually, the villagers' sympathy for the family's loss became resentment, and the family was blamed for being the reason why their village had not been developed faster, why the access road wasn't constructed earlier, and why the tourism of their area wasn't promoted more widely.

Long after 'Uongu's execution, throughout Florence's childhood and youth, she witnessed her family members being obliged to fill out all kinds of forms, apply for all kinds of permissions, write down all kinds of self-statements, and answer all kinds of inquiries from law enforcement, even if they were just visiting their relatives in the next village, going to school in the next county, or simply sending produce from their farm to friends. When Florence's cousin Tibusungu, 'Uongu's oldest grandson, was leaving home to attend a junior college in Chiayi City, the entire family was worried that he would be bullied, either by the so called "special agents" watching them all the time, or by people from the city who might have learned the history of his family.

Florence grew up surrounded by the fear instilled in her grandparents and parents, but with no one to explain to her what they were really afraid of, or why. When Martial Law was finally abolished in 1987, and the surveillance over their community gradually withdrew, the fears remained. They had long lost their motivation and mobility to travel, to make new friends, or to explore different things in life. They were too intimidated to do anything beyond their daily routine; a disability grew up in their minds, stopping them from being more curious or ambitious.

Over the thirty-five years between 'Uongu's death and the end of Martial Law, Florence's grandaunt, 'Uongu's wife, died, and her grandpa Yaipuku died. When the "special agents" who were always in black suits finally disappeared from their community, Florence's grandma mocked them in bitterness, "Those guys will never find another occupation. All these years they cultivated no profession beyond honing their skills of threatening ordinary people. They are no good for anything."

In the following decades after Martial Law, research regarding 'Uongu and his activism started, and the few images of his short life could be found online. Looking at the young profile of her granduncle, Florence saw that everyone affected by his death had aged much more than he had. The cruelty of the political oppression in the past was not only about the sudden termination of his life, but the hopelessness and solitude slowly sprawling across and suffocating their family.

***

One afternoon Florence walked out from a pedicure service and saw the man who had followed her shortly after she handed money to a young woman the other day. Florence looked around and as expected, she saw the same young woman. Was she on another mission? Florence was good at spotting her watcher, in the way she had been trained. The "special agents" invariably were faceless, characterless and relentless. She waited for a while until both the woman and her watcher took off, and entered the bookstore she liked to stop by.

After browsing the bookshelves for a moment, Florence approached the counter and addressed the young man with a pair of big eyeglasses who was serving there, "Do you have *An Act of Terror* by André Brink?"

"Yes." The young man got up on his feet and led Florence to a bookshelf labeled "International Literature" at the back of an aisle. When the man lifted his arm to pull out a novel with a black-and-white cover, Florence quickly inserted an envelope into the pocket of the apron he wore.

"You do know that the girl who just took off is under surveillance, don't you?" Florence flipped over the book and spoke in a low voice, pretending she was inquiring about the book's content.

"Yes."

"Be extremely cautious, otherwise you will be watched, too."

"Yes. Thanks," The young man expressed his appreciation and then his despair, "When will all this end?"

"It took us 50 years." As soon as Florence responded, she regretted it, for she saw the same helplessness of her family in the young man's eyes. She added immediately, "But you don't have to struggle for that long. We had been isolated and misled, but you are not. If everyone does something she or he is able to, we will make changes much sooner."

They walked toward the cashier together, and Florence paid for the book with her credit card. As the young man nodded to her solemnly, Florence couldn't help but imagine how this young man would look when he was in his seventies, and how her granduncle would have looked if he had made it to his seventies. She prayed that the young man, along with all others in the struggle, did not have the fate of 'Uongu.

Originally published by *Mocking Owl Roost Literary Magazine*

I Am Not Broken

I had my 26th birthday "celebrated" with my friends. They were unusual characters so they could be with me in this small place. They were ghosts. I was so grateful for their presence when my human friends were unable to join me for the celebration. I had been arrested many times and had been in and out of prison over the past years, and since two years ago, this prison became my home. I spent my 25th birthday in the same place, by myself, although my friends and supporters outside had sent their good wishes during those days.

Then I encountered my ghost friends. They appeared one by one, three in total, at different times. They don't know each other, and they never appear at the same time. I asked them if it was possible for them to show up at the same time, but they seem to have different times in their worlds, so I have problems setting up an appointment with all of them. They stopped by at different times, but they all made it on my birthday.

I knew Kimura first, he showed up by the basketball court during one of the very rare opportunities I was given to exercise outdoors. I thought he was waiting for our game to be over so he could play, but he did not approach when my game was over. I played another game, and when it was time for me to go back to my cell, I gestured that he could take my place, but he did not respond.

Several days later, I saw him during meal time. We did not interact. I knew I was closely watched, so I avoided bringing unnecessary trouble to strangers, until one night he showed up in my cell. I was surprised and thought he must be a prison staff, not an inmate, so he could get in the cell. He did not say anything, just sat down by the desk and read something.

"Hey!" I called.

He lifted up his head and nodded to me, then continued his reading.

"Who are you?" I inquired, noticing the uniform he wore was different to ours or that of the prison staff. It was white shirt, khaki shorts and leggings. He slowly lifted his head and told me his name was Kimura, and he was from Kempeitai.

"What is Kempeitai?"

Kimura did not answer. Instead he stood up and

came to sit next to me, on my bed, without being invited, "I am twenty-three years old, how old are you?"

"Twenty-five." I was a little bit surprised that his unexpected movement and question did not annoy me.

"You are two years older than me. Did you go to school?"

"Yes, I was attending Hong Kong Metropolitan University before… before I was taken here. I did not finish my degree."

"Me, either." Kimura said, "I was drafted when I just started college."

"If you have the chance in the future, will you complete your study?" I asked without really wishing to know the answer. Just trying to find a topic for a chat.

"Nay. I never had the chance." Kimura replied, he looked lost. "You study by yourself a lot, can I study with you?"

"Of course." I promised without thinking, but wondered how. Kimura seemed to be happy, and faded away while saying, "I will come back again."

The next ghost becoming my friend was Joshua, "I am Joshua, can I share the table with you?" A middle aged man inquired politely, like we were in a high-end bar, instead of being in a prison.

"Yes, please. I am Joshua, too." I saw him two times before he introduced himself. He was in the corridor of our cellblock, he wore a formal suit and tie, and carried a black leather suitcase. Usually it caused loud echoes when anyone walked past the corridor, but this man never produced any sound. Based on my acquaintance with Kimura, when Joshua asked to share the table with me, I realized he was a ghost, too.

From our conversation, I learned that Joshua was a philosopher. He became my tutor in the following encounters and taught me scientific analysis of philosophic, moral, legal and social issues. Out of respect, I called him Dr. Liao, but he insisted on being called Joshua, so I called him Dr. Joshua. And when Kimura visited me, I taught him what I had learned from Dr. Joshua, although sometimes I was confused by different theories I learned. Repeating what Dr. Joshua had taught me to Kimura helped me clarify what I really understood, and what I needed to further pursue in the coming classes provided by Dr. Joshua.

As if my behavior interacting with ghosts was not crazy enough, the third friend showed up not long after Dr. Liao. It was a little blond boy with fair skin, probably three years old, similar to the build of my cousin's child. He played by himself around me from time to time, barely able to talk. I described the appearance of the boy to Kimura, and he said, "It must be Brian." Kimura told me Brian was taken here when he was around three years old, when Japan occupied British Hong Kong. He died of malnutrition when he was almost four years old. I was told that his grave was just outside of my cell, "He probably doesn't know he is dead." Kimura assumed.

"Ah! No wonder. The little boy always looks like he was expecting someone or something. Poor thing. What happened to his parents?"

"I am not sure. They might have died, too, or have been released afterwards and returned to the UK. I don't remember his parents."

"How about you, Kimura? How did you die?" I finally raised the question I had in my mind since I met him.

"I was hanged."

I couldn't hide my shock, so Kimura explained, "We tortured and murdered Hong Kong civilians during the war. Brian was one of them. We were sentenced to death in the trials after the war"

"You tortured and murdered Brian?" I asked, unbelievably.

"Not directly. I followed the orders from my superiors. I was at the lowest rank, I did what they told me to do."

A thousand questions rushed over my mind, and Kimura seemed to be understanding, "I was numb when I was executing my orders. The prisoners were asked to stand under the scorching sun for hours, or to be starved for days. When one made a mistake, we punished all of them. We did not see those people punished by us as humans."

"I see. We were not treated as humans when we were beaten up in the streets by the law enforcement, either. The police called us cockroaches."

Kimura was buried in the mass grave outside of the prison, he hung out in the screwpine woods a lot and seemed to be much more carefree in nature. No one except me in this prison was able to see him, and neither of us knew why. I wondered if he missed his hometown in Japan, and, as a ghost, was he able to go home.

I had heard quite a few ghost stories about this prison established in 1937, and it indeed was haunted, considering the three friends of mine. But they were not scary at all. People operating this prison were scarier. Prisoners executed here a long time ago were buried in the mass grave, their families were not allowed to have burials until seven years later. Many were not reburied at all, Kimura was one of the unclaimed souls.

The next time when Dr. Joshua came, I boldly asked the cause of his death.

"I was poisoned, although the newspapers said I was killed by a cerebral hemorrhage. I was only 46 years old, it's very unlikely I'd die by a brain hemorrhage, but it was the official story."

"Why did they want to poison you?"

"I was campaigning for Taiwan's independence from China."

"I see. It had been a taboo forever…until recently."

I told him about the other two ghosts who died several years before his death, Dr. Joshua was amazed. Obviously he did not hear much about it. He inquired a lot about them but I couldn't answer, I promised him that next time when Kimura showed up, I would ask him. As to Brian, I suspected his extended term in the prison had resulted in delayed development of his communication skills. I felt so sorry for him and his parents.

Each inmate is allowed to have six books a month. They are usually brought to me by my family or friends when they have the chance to visit. Prisoner visitation is highly inconvenient here; visitors often need to wait for hours for a brief 15-minute meeting. The prison administration isn't here to serve us. I always ask my family and friends to bring publications related to Dr. Joshua's classes, but many of them are very old and no longer available. My family and friends try to find books with themes as close to my studies as possible, and I show them to Dr. Joshua when he is with me.

I have always been curious about how a ghost updates his knowledge. Can Dr. Joshua exchange thoughts with the ghosts of other philosophers? I raised this question, and Dr. Joshua told me that in the world he inhabits now, the being of each individual is not tangible, thus the interactions between them are not like those in my world. I don't fully understand what this means; perhaps it is the so-called metaphysics?

As the next date of the trial of my next lawsuit approaches, I get more and more unsettled. I am charged with "violation of the anti-mask law", "organizing an unauthorized assembly", "promoting secession or subversion" and "contempt of court". I have been told there could be further charges brought in the future. I remember that several weeks ago I discovered that my name had been linked to a former activist, who was found guilty of corruption for misappropriating funds he had raised for public affairs. The report implied that I was involved in the scandal as well, although I hardly worked with the man in question. I was depressed, but couldn't do anything. Fortunately Dr. Joshua showed up, I told him what bothered me.

"It's normal. One of their common methods to stigmatize political dissidents."

I hesitated a moment, and asked, "What else?"

"I don't know about your situation, certainly it couldn't be as bad as mine. You already knew I was poisoned, and my siblings and my cousins were put in jail for the longest time. To save them from being sentenced to death, my younger brother went back to Taiwan from Japan and surrendered himself to the Nationalist regime. He was used for propaganda as proof of how evil the conspiracy for Taiwan's independence was, while my entire family was still under surveillance and humiliation for decades. Had my siblings known the price of confession was deprivation of our dignity, they'd persist."

I looked at him for a long time, and finally said, "Your spirit came here to warn me?"

"I don't know why I am here. I respect you greatly. You could be my child, and thinking what might happen to my own offspring, I struggle, it hurts me. Should I support them to do what they are doing, or should I advise them to compromise for an easier life, I have no idea. But I am confident that with more allies and supporters to support your voice, you certainly will see your achievement in a shorter period of time compared to mine, and your efforts will be recognized widely."

I felt I was wrapped by warm and chilly streams of air at the same time. When Dr. Joshua was gone, I stood up, closed my eyes and began to jog in my cell.

I imagined myself running in a prairie, it was so expansive that no border could be envisaged, and the breeze kissed my hair, my forehead, my arms and my torso, like I was embraced by a tender giant.

Author's Note:
Joshua Wong, a Hong Kong pro-democracy activist, has sent a message, through his allies, from the Stanley Prison after his 26th birthday, that he is not broken, even after more than two years of incarceration and faced with more charges and trials.

Originally published by *Diversity of Voices:
A Global Storytelling History*

In Your Eyes, I See

In your eyes, bro, I see anger, despair, and determination.

But please. Please do not approach the line any more. I don't want to confront you with my baton. I don't want to see you hurt by pepper spray.

I don't want to report to my supervisors again and again, about the forces I have applied. I don't want to explain to reporters, prosecutors and judges again and again what methods I chose to defend law and order during the conflicts.

I don't want to beat you up in front of my colleagues.

***

In your eyes, dear, I see sorrow and hesitation.

But please. Please stay away from our demonstration. I don't want to be your enemy, for you are one of us.

I am tired of criticizing you as the tool of our oppressors. I am tired of pointing my finger at you, a victim of the system that you are defending. I am tired of seeing you pretend you are doing fine in your position.

I am tired of being a sympathizer of your dilemma.

***

In your eyes, bro, I see regret and uncertainty.

Please, go home. Your voices are heard, things will be better tomorrow. Go home, stay with your wife and children, they have had enough of your relentless activism. More turmoil is not going to save our world.

***

In your eyes, dear, I see fear and compromise.

Please, back out. Admit your effort to make any change on your part is futile.

Don't you understand the system is using you and exploiting you by placing you in it?

***

In your/my eyes, I/you see traumas of being discriminated against, wounds of being deprived with our languages, histories, traditions and cultural heritages.

In my/your eyes, you/I see our shared history of blood shedding and ongoing suffering from state violence and injustice.

Please, be cool, man.

Sing our heavenly songs, chant our poems passed on to us by our parents, grandparents, and great grandparents. Say prayers to our ancestral spirits.

If we are powerless to solve the cruel opposition between us, remember we have inherited love and respect for one another.

If there is no place for us to stand together, remember we are born with dignity, live with dignity and die with dignity.

In my/your eyes, you/I see me/you.

Political Prisoners

Walking one hundred circles in the 13-square-meter cell after lunch. There are four of us, and in such a small room, every one of us must walk at the same time, in a file.

We put our bowls on a stool, each time we walk past the bowls, we put a crumb of the tasteless bun in one of the bowls. When all the bowls contain 25 crumbs, we are done with the walking. It takes us a little more than one hour.

"I am not in the mood to walk." No. 639 says.

"You must. Because we are." No.726 responds.

"I wish I would die." No. 639 says.

"You are not. As a traitor in the eyes of the nation, you don't control when you die." No. 597 retorts. Based on the number, we know he is the most senior prisoner in our cell. No one of us knows how much time the others have been here, and how much longer each of us will remain.

No one of us knows why each of us is here. We

don't talk about it because we know we are being watched.

No. 639 stands up, unwillingly joining the walking file.

"It's for your good," I say in a low voice, "we must live longer than the dictator. We must survive his regime."

It is one of the things we do everyday to pretend we are still hopeful. We are No.597, No. 639, No. 726 and No. 774. We are political prisoners.

Originally published by *Edge of Humanity*

Prison Break

The thirteenth month. Late autumn.

The roughly hewn walls are damp, with patches of mold and fungus growing in the crevices. Water stains streak down, and the air is heavy with the scent of mildew and decay. The bricks are discolored, their edges slicked by humidity. The dank, musty atmosphere lurks in every corner of the cell, sprawling to the skin and weighing down the spirits of the people living within.

These walls bear witness to the despair and suffering of those who ever had been confined in them, generation after generation. They hold their memories; hope, fear, determination, and regret. Their fabric is so coarse and patchy, it seems to seep in each man's unfortunate personal history.

The thirty-seventh month. Is it spring?

Tiny ferns break through and grow out of the crevices on the walls. Their delicate fronds, in vibrant green, fan out like miniature umbrellas, waving gently in the rare breeze blown from the high window. Their stems are slender and wiry, weaving in and out of the cracks in the walls.

I was a journalist, and I am a political prisoner, for my freedom-of-speech and anti-authoritarian-regime campaign. I lost almost all contact with the outside world, and don't know how much longer I will be here.

I imagine the ferns clinging tenaciously to the rough surface of my cell, their roots burrowing deep into the cracks, and eventually shattering down the walls.

These ferns are my will of survival, my prison break.

Author's Note:

According to the Reporters Without Borders (Reporters Sans Frontieres, or RSF), as of 2024, there are 550 media professionals imprisoned all over the world. China remains the biggest jailer of journalists(124, including 11 in Hong Kong), followed by Myanmar(61), Israel(41) and Russia(38).

Originally published by *Flash Fiction*

He and Darkness Become One

I.

He sits on the bed most of the time, as if listening intently, though there is no sound. He hardly moves, and as daylight fades, his profile is gradually swallowed by the darkness behind him.

There are always three books on his desk. Each inmate can borrow three books a month, and he always finishes them in the first week. Sometimes he reads them twice, but even so, it takes very little time.

I was told he was a publisher before he was jailed. He must have read a lot more books in the past. The books here don't satisfy him; they are cliché.

He must hear something that calms him. No one can sit like that for hours, for days, for months, and for years. From the door, he seems like a single note on sheet music. I read him as a slow melody played on a piano with one finger. Over time, it becomes a moving song, a masterpiece, a symbol of eternity.

But no one appreciates eternity in prison.

II.

He just stares at the blank wall. He is not meditating, he is not thinking. But if he is not thinking, how is he called a thought criminal?

He is waiting. During the day, he waits for night; at night, he waits for sunrise. He waits for the short walks allowed twice a day in the yard. He waits for meals that provide nothing but tasteless food. He waits for the two visits per month when he can meet his friends. His family has fallen apart.

Perhaps he isn't staring at the wall; he just looks into the blankness of the air. I was told he has never been tried, thus he cannot openly defend himself in court.

He begins to write. He asks for paper and pens and is given a very short pencil to prevent it from being used as a weapon. He writes something no one understands, and some say it is poetry. He is asked to read his poetry for us, and he does so by the high window, under the weak starlight, after the lights are out before bedtime.

It is the only time we hear him, otherwise, he almost doesn't speak at all. He reads in a tender tone, as if telling bedtime stories to his daughter. Sometimes he reads new works, sometimes he repeats old ones. I often fall asleep during his readings because I don't understand his poems.

One day, he is moved. No one knows where he has gone. We never saw him again. It is said he wasn't able to bring his poems with him; the prison officers burned them. It is a pity, although we cannot judge whether his writing was good or bad. A thought criminal is not allowed to express himself.

But inexplicably, I found myself able to remember and recite many of his poems in my head. I begin to hear what he heard, see what he saw in the night. The darkness shrouds me, we also become one.

Originally published by *Hooghly Review*

Glossary for the Trial of National Security Law in Hong Kong

Your Honor:

The term "Anti-structure" I used in my news report comes from political theories. It refers to a sociocultural structure that intentionally counteracts the mainstream. Yes, it is what I do, and what I encourage my fellow activists to do.

When I used the term "dead end," I was referring to the hopelessness people feel about the implementation of the National Security Law. I was also referring to the symbolic system of elections that never conveys people's wishes.

The term "totalitarianism" I mentioned in my comment suggests the regime's total control of society through strict censorship, surveillance, and persecution of dissenters. Your Honor, you know as well as I do the answer to whether we are living under totalitarianism. I, a journalist accused of attempting to subvert the nation simply by revealing the truth, am undeniable proof of totalitarianism.

No, Your Honor, I do not plead guilty.

Do I have the "freedom" to apply legal approaches to express my opinions? Your Honor, when something is legal in other democratic countries but not legal here, or when something was legal before but not legal now, we don't have "freedom." A person in a free society doesn't have to bypass political landmines with caution. Your Honor, as you sit on the bench now, trying all means to convict me under the political pressure on your shoulders, without considering any possibility to acquit me, you are not a free man, either.

No, Your Honor, I am not submitting a mitigation plea. I have no remorse for what I have done, and I have nothing to repent.

No, Your Honor, I don't campaign for militant activism. All the actions we take are simply reactions to the state violence we face.

No, Your Honor, if our debate here is for you to find reasons not to be remembered for your servitude to power, then you are the one seeking a mitigation plea from history and people's memory.

Author's Note:
Gwyneth Ho, a Hong Kong journalist and pro-democracy

activist, is incarcerated on the charge of "attempting to subvert the nation." During her trial, she refused to plead guilty and did not file a mitigation plea for leniency. She faces a maximum penalty of life imprisonment.

Bookstore Owners in Hong Kong

You own a bookstore, so you may be considered a suspect of collusion with external elements to endanger national security, based on the sale of the publications by foreign writers.

You own a bookstore that sells politically sensitive publications, so you might be suspected of committing secession or undermining national unification. The evidence is the protests against the government by your customers.

You own a bookstore which also publishes books, so you could be a suspect of participating in acts by force or threat of force or other unlawful means to subvert the state power. The evidence is the organized activism of your readers.

You own a bookstore which also publishes politically sensitive books, so you must be a suspect of threatening to commit terrorist activities causing or intended to cause grave harm to the society. The evidence is the dissident voices of your authors.

You own a bookstore and you are the author of politically sensitive books, so you are no doubt a suspect involving crimes of treason and other offenses against national security.

The evidence is the resistant ideas conveyed in your work.

Under a dictatorship, a bookstore is perceived as an arsenal, and books are ammunition. Each word in the books is a bullet capable of penetrating the walls of thought.

You own a bookstore and you are condemned, because you are a bigger threat to the regime than an army.

Author's Note:

In Hong Kong, many bookstore owners, particularly those who were also authors or publishers, have faced persecution by the Chinese authoritarian regime. They have been imprisoned and coerced into confessing their alleged intention to subvert the regime. Some of them relocated their bookstores to other cities, some were forced to close down their establishments, and others continue to face ongoing struggles.

Handbook of Conflict Avoidance

"We tried to obtain our rights to education and independence through reasoning, but instead, we were punished," said the Iranian women.

"We tried to effect changes in the ruling power through elections, but in this country, such a thing does not exist," said pro-democracy Hong Kong detainees.

"We tried to stop government corruption by disclosing information, but we got ourselves in trouble," said the indicted journalists.

"We tried to express our love of peace in an anti-war march, but the march was brutally cracked down," said the incarcerated Russian dissidents.

"We tried to mitigate climate disasters by preserving our territories, but no one listens," said indigenous communities.

"We tried to earn the respect of society by becoming model citizens, but we are still suspects of every crime," said African Americans.

"We tried to be left in peace by obeying the regime, but we ended up in genocide," said Uyghurs.

"We tried to appease the aggressor by dissuading some countries' membership application, but it did not stop the invasion," said NATO.

"We tried to remain blind to the injustices inflicted on others for our own survival, but we only hastened our own victimhood," said us.

Originally published by *Poetica Review*

Freedom of Sp.e..e...c...
What did you say?

Paper Submitted from
Dr. Denise Ho
Mr. _____
Ms. _____

Submission Date
Jan 20, 2022

Institute
National Yang Ming University, Taiwan

Academic Field
☐ Arts
☐ Architecture
☐ History
☐ Law
☐ Philosophy
■ Political Science
☐ Social Science

☐ Sociology
☐ Urban Planning

Title of Paper
The Disappeared Freedom of Speech in Hong Kong: One and Half Years of the Enforcement of the National Security Law

Abstract

The implementation of the National Security Law on Hong Kong in July 2020 kicked off strict censorship on speech and draconian regulations over the operation of news media. *Apple Daily* stopped printing its newspaper in June, 2021, after its founder and executives were arrested and its assets frozen. In August, 2021, *Initium Media*, established in 2015, moved its administrative office from Hong Kong to Singapore. Independent journalist media outlet *Stand News*, which was founded after the Umbrella Movement, ended its business after its headquarters was ransacked by police and its board members and editors were detained on 29 December, 2021. Later the *Citizen News* announced its closure in January, 2022, due to its concern for the safety of its staff. *Citizen News* only operated for five years in Hong Kong.

The oppression of journalistic freedom in Hong

Kong is compared to the White Terror of Taiwan. During the White Terror period, all publications and speech were censored, all remarks criticising policies and the authorities were filtered out, and political dissidents were silenced by brutal measures, including secret arrests, executions without trial, and close surveillance, among others.

This study also looks back at how the nationalist regime in Taiwan tightened its control over the society by restraining sensitive topics and implanting propaganda through state supported media, and to the possible future for Hong Kong through the experience of Taiwan's decades of struggle for freedom of speech and the ultimate goal of democratization.

Keywords: Hong Kong, Taiwan, Freedom of Speech, National Security Law, Umbrella Movement, Apple Daily, Stand News, Citizen News, Initium Media, White Terror

***

Reviewer 2 of this paper, Prof. Robert Burton read through the paper first, then checked the references before reading it again. The author referred to many online links from these news media outlets which were no longer in business. He clicked the links but in many of them he saw message:

This page is no longer available

How was he to judge the quality of this paper under the situation in which he couldn't find the sources of the author's references? Prof. Burton was given the task of reviewing this paper because he was an expert of East Asian Studies. He had lived in Hong Kong and taught in the Hong Kong Chinese University for four years. His son was born in Hong Kong twenty years ago. Over the past years he had kept close watch over Hong Kong's political turmoils, and the development concerned him tremendously. Those activists in Hong Kong were so young, most of them were about the age of his son, but except for traffic offenses, his son who had moved to the US never had to worry about being arrested for what he had said, whom he had met, or what he was planning to do.

Prof. Burton went to the front page to find the conclusion of the comments from reviewer 1, it read:

> This well structured paper has successfully achieved the goal in delineating the current political climate in Hong Kong, as well as the sim-

ilarities and different conditions between today's Hong Kong and the past Taiwan.

Many of the author's references correctly proved the situation of the disappeared dissidents and deprived freedom of speech in Hong Kong, making the publication of this paper especially significant at this moment.

Prof. Burton contemplated on the comment of the reviewer 1 for a moment, he felt an invisible bond forming between the author, himself, and his unknown fellow reviewer. He realized that reviewer 1 must have thought the missing links happened to provide evidence of the worsening situation in Hong Kong. He had to agree. The paper was well written, and the author has no need to make up what she had found earlier from the referred links.

History repeats, but the academic bureaucracy should not, thought Prof. Burton. He decided to suggest the journal editors publish this article. These issues should be always brought up to the world, so people in Hong Kong wouldn't have to endure the deprivation of human rights and democracy they demanded, as well as suffering isolation Taiwanese people had over the past decades. What can present stronger proof of the lost freedom of speech than the missing news reports?

Un(found) Poetry—A Fiction

I.

Dear Esteemed Contributors,

I hope this message finds you well. I would like to take a moment to express my deep appreciation for the insightful and thought-provoking columns you have contributed to our newsletter. Your dedication to journalistic excellence continues to uphold our reputation as a pioneer of information and analysis.

As you craft your future columns, I kindly remind you to be mindful of the current socio-political climate. It is important that our content remains respectful and considerate of the broader context in which we operate. I trust you will exercise your best judgment in navigating complex topics with the sensitivity and discretion that you have consistently demonstrated.

Please continue to focus on issues that resonate

with our readers, highlighting stories of resilience, innovation, and community. By doing so, we can contribute positively to the public discourse while maintaining the integrity and safety of our work.

Thank you once again for your unwavering commitment and professionalism. I look forward to reading your upcoming contributions.

Warm regards,

Editor-in-Chief
Liu Sung-Yang
Ming Newspaper, Hong Kong

II.
Dear Mr. Meng,

Your prose poem has been accepted. The editorial office will notify you of the publication date. Please keep in mind that the newspaper reserves the right to edit accepted works.

Born ~~on June 4th~~

In the hushed darkness of summer nights, we gather, candles in hand, flickering beacons against the void. Each year, a vigil for those silenced ~~on June~~

~~4th~~. Each flame a soul, their number unknown. Each whisper a name, consigned to history's ashes.

~~The regime deemed our candles a threat, our memories a peril~~. Year after year, the light grew dimmer, the space around us emptier. Yet, as your existence is engraved, my brothers and sisters in the free square ~~of '89~~, so are our spirits.

~~Now, the vigil is forbidden, the square a forsaken land~~. How much longer can they endure in our fading memories? How do we inhale the air of ~~illusional~~ freedom and exhale the essence of truth?

In this place, in this era, ~~the survivors wear their shame~~. Happy birthday to those reborn ~~on June 4th~~.

Our Burials at Sea

Rumor has it that we perished while attempting to flee this colony of injustice and oppression, a place intertwined with our personal history and memories. Unfortunately, a hurricane struck just after we set sail, casting us into the jaws of ravenous waves. Our bodies were torn apart and devoured by fish.

Another rumor claims we were killed trying to escape the suffocating autocracy. Tragically, we were shot dead on the boat by rifles fired from the shore, never even getting the chance to unfurl our sail. Our bodies sank into the sea, our blood stained the water red momentarily.

Yet another rumor suggests we died while sailing northeast toward an island fraught with conflict and risk, but also full of promise. Sadly, we became lost in the boundless sea. Day turned to night and night to day, our ignorance of the constellations failing us. Exhausted from fresh water and food, we succumbed to dehydration.

All these rumors paint a more merciful fate than the truth. In reality, before we even tasted the salty water, we were handcuffed on land and thrown into jail. In solitary confinement, deprived of fresh air and natural light, our wills decayed, and our minds drifted in the torturous dungeon. Our souls, lingering at the seashore, slowly faded into oblivion.

Author's Note:

In August 2020, twelve Hong Kong pro-democracy protestors, charged under the National Security Law and on probation, were arrested when their speedboat was intercepted by the China Coast Guard. They were attempting to flee to Taiwan.

Rest, Not In Peace

When you see this post, I've logged out from this world.

The news media claimed I had suffered from stress and depression for a long time due to my academic career. It's a lie.

In my last will, I made it clear that my despair began in 2019, after the tragic political storm. Aren't we all victims of state violence with our dissident status?

I regret having to say farewell to my beloved city, the once dynamic Hong Kong: its crazy traffic, incredible street food, maze-like roads, sky-blocking high-rise buildings, and diverse populations—from the show-off rich to the hard-working poor, from natives whose ancestors settled here generations ago to immigrants with indiscernible accents. But what I miss most is the free air. Free to express, free to fall in love, free to dream, free to sing, and free to leave and return.

All these are gone now. In our twenties, we witnessed our fellow students killed during the brutal crackdown in Beijing. The whole generation of us was wiped out. And thirty-five years later, we still failed to pass on a free society to our students in their twenties. We are losing them to relentless authoritarianism.

I am so tired of living in fear, fear for myself as well as for those I hold dear. I am afraid I can't restrain my resentment to the political propaganda, or my criticism of the power. I am afraid of my memories of the past, the haunting spirits of my college classmates and the ghost of my hidden identity. I am afraid of my sense of loss, the glory and shame in life.

My hopelessness is heavy; in fact, heavier each day. I am no longer able to carry it. So I decided to confront it, to terminate it.

I suppose having my body shattered by a train must feel like being run over by a tank.

My dear fellow Hong Kongers, may my legacy become the fuel for your resistance. I hope you all see the light at the end of the tunnel soon. As for me, I shall not rest in peace, I rest in anger.

Author's Note:

On August 25, 2024, Professor Li Hin-Wa of the City University in Hong Kong jumped onto the tracks at Kowloon Tong Station and took his own life. This prose is based on his ambiguous suicide note. "I suppose having my body shattered by a train must feel like being run over by a tank" is a translated quote from the note. In 2019, two million Hong Kong residents protested against the Extradition Bill, which, rather than targeting criminals, aimed at political dissidents. Nevertheless, the CCP's control over thought has since become increasingly stringent.

Originally published by *Cigarette Fire Magazine*

I Died Three Years Ago

I moved to the US from Hong Kong three years ago, with a fake identity and a disguised appearance.

When Albert and Anne, the owners of Autumn Light Bookstore, realized that their bookstore would eventually become a target of the draconian National Security Law, they knew they had to take action. During this time, many independent news outlets were raided and shut down, and bookstores were being accused of spreading materials that disrupted social harmony.

Anne was an urban planner working with architects in Hong Kong. When she started the job, her husband Albert, a New York attorney, moved to Asia with her. Albert's grandparents were from Hong Kong, so moving there was a kind of nostalgic adventure to him. They were happy with their move and celebrated their new life in Hong Kong. They rented an affordable place on the 27th floor of an industrial building to set up their bookstore—

Albert's dream since he was a child—and gradually built up their reputation through word-of-mouth recommendations from book lovers.

In the third year of Autumn Light Bookstore, the political climate in Hong Kong took a drastic turn. As China tightened its control over local matters, including representative democracy, educational curriculum, and freedom of speech, young people began to openly express their opposition. Student movements were very common in the US, so Albert and Anne supported the young people by displaying their banners over the door of Autumn Light, printing and giving away stickers for demonstrations, and participating in student parades whenever they had time. For three consecutive summers, they joined the candlelight vigil for the 1989 massacre in Beijing. They never imagined that all these activities would become illegal and subject to violent crackdowns.

During the demonstrations of tens of thousands of protesters, I was one of the unfortunate individuals arrested. After days of torture in the sweatbox, I was finally released, after my mother had spent a whole week searching for my whereabouts.

Following my temporary release, I decided to leave Hong Kong with Autumn Light Bookstore. With the help of my fellow activists, I obtained a fake identity and a new look. I was no longer who I was, but I successfully broke away from the police surveillance. I had to live with my phantom-like self.

The relocation of Autumn Light took Albert and Anne a couple of years. They held sales for the books they couldn't take with them and packed the unsold books along with all their belongings accumulated over six years in Hong Kong. I lingered with them, but like a banned book, I must be hidden.

After arriving in the US, they still needed to move around to find a home for their bookstore. After a wild search, they finally settled down in a suburb of Seattle, thanks to the enthusiastic support of local communities.

I followed them and stayed with them, and in their bookstore, I moved from bookshelf to bookshelf, as if the Autumn Light were my home, consisting of my living quarters and bedroom. I still can't use my real identity because my mother had claimed my death since I "disappeared" again three years ago.

It has been three years since my death, so I am no longer legal and identifiable. My ghostly being is coverless and unrecognizable. Still, I am haunting, like a banned, unreadable book that is moved around in a persisting bookstore.

I Am Lucky, A Cat

I cautiously step over piles of rubble and debris, navigating through the remnants of buildings. The air is thick with dust, and the acrid smell of smoke and burning fills my nostrils. Jagged metal scraps and glass shards litter the ground, casting shadows in the muted light.

I scan the scene of destruction and chaos—fallen walls and bricks, broken columns and pipes, distorted windows and doors. I see through the gloom, and the movement of my prey stands out against the stillness of the ruins. I notice there are broken pieces of furniture, shredded curtains, and mangled metal frames scattering around the area. My ears twitch as I hear sounds of rubble shifting, and cries from a distance.

Night begins to fall, the smell of smoke lightens a little, but the air still thickens as things gradually dismantle. I seem to hear sirens afar, and desperate wails of survivors. Or are they just my imagination?

I wander into the darkened city, once populated and thriving, now evacuated due to the war. A piece of broken mirror glints, reflecting the starlight from the darkening sky. I walk over to check myself and realize that my fur is covered with dust. I shake violently to get rid of it.

I must find a shelter before it gets colder, it might snow anytime. I creep into a small alleyway and by a fallen brickwall I found a cardboard box, which makes a perfect bed. I will try to find some food left by evacuees when the first light of dawn appears.

I am a feral cat in the city. Throughout my life I am on my own. Before the war, my life was quite carefree. I had no problems finding good food, and I could always find cozy places to sleep. I enjoyed great freedom. I was satisfied, triumphant, and even elegant. I was a nocturnal creature; I belonged to the night, and the night belonged to me. I loved to walk over shadows cast by lamplights, listen to cars roaring by once in a while, or drunkards singing in happiness or shouting in despair. Sounds of showers or toilets flushing gave away undisclosable romances or untold sleepless nights. In smaller lanes, low volumes of music or restrained quarrels echoed in the corridors or community atria. Everything yet nothing could be hidden at night.

A predatory element was still strong in my character, but I wasn't one to catch rodents, birds or raccoons. I might chase them for the thrill of it, but catching them was not my goal. I was after the life stories of humans.

A street cat in the city, I often found myself hanging around bookstores. There's nothing quite like dozing off by a sunlit window on a winter afternoon. One time, while wandering through the aisles of the Causeway Bell Bookstore, I stumbled upon a cozy corner nestled between the sociology and literary theory sections. This area was usually deserted, with few customers venturing this far back.

Although I can't read, I do enjoy judging books by their readers. On this particular day, a man wearing a fedora and brown check coat was browsing through a thick tome by the bookshelf. I enjoyed the sound of the pages rustling as he turned them. I knew this man well—he wasn't quite who he appeared to be and often visited Causeway Bell for secret errands. However, he was also a serious reader, often purchasing one or two books during each visit. Despite his mysterious ways, he never bothered me while I napped nearby.

It was tricky to run an independent bookstore in this city, especially for a bookstore that also served as an independent publisher. Causeway Bell had rich collections of history, urban planning, political science, sociology, poetry and fiction. And for familiar and trusted customers, Causeway Bell was the go-to spot for banned books. As a result, the bookstore was often subject to police searches, with the owner or staff being taken away for interrogation. I gave them a warning when I sensed that law enforcement was on the move, I think it was the reason why I was not bothered when taking naps in the bookstore. We freedom lovers look after one another.

I kept secrets for people. For example, I knew Martin, the man in his forties and a high-ranking official of the state-owned gas company, was taking kickbacks from the businesses that the gas company made procurements with. On the second Wednesday night of each month, there would be men stopping by his apartment on G street. The visits usually were very short, and they talked in very low voices. I could jump to the windowpane of his living room to observe them. Martin would take a box, or an envelope, or a bag from his visitors without checking it when they were around, and if I stayed on the windowpane long enough, I'd see him count the money after his visitors took off, and where he put it away. Then he carefully burned the envelope or box or bag in the fireplace.

Martin was a homely man. He lived in a simple

apartment, dressed plainly, carried a plain briefcase and drove a modest car to work. I had no idea why he needed so much money, and how he spent it. His wife and two children led ordinary lives, shopping at budget supermarkets and attending public schools. Knowing where Martin hid his money was useless to me, but the food he and his family left behind when they ran away from war had sustained me for quite a while. Martin couldn't bring all the ill-gained wealth with him, as he and his wife had to take care of their two children and the belongings they could use during their relocation. Martin and his family expected to come back soon, as everyone hoped the war wouldn't last long.

Catherine and her husband Leo were at odds over the doors of their new home. Catherine insisted on wooden doors, but Leo objected, citing the high cost of wood and suggesting stainless steel as a more affordable option. Catherine, however, found stainless steel to be unappealing. Despite Leo's compromise of having wooden doors for the exterior and stainless steel for the interior, Catherine remained unsatisfied, believing that mixing materials would ruin the taste of their home. Both Catherine and Leo were stubborn in their convictions, and their disagreements caused tension between them. As the argument escalated, they began to quarrel about other matters they had previously agreed upon, and their families joined in on the fighting. Little did they know, there were high-quality pre-owned wooden doors available at the Public Building Material Bank, an institute dedicated to the restoration of historical sites which provided the option of purchasing materials salvaged from demolished buildings. Had they and their relatives spent less time trying to win the quarrels, they'd discover the solutions.

Now everything has been turned to ash. Books from Causeway Bell Bookstore were taken and burned by people seeking warmth on cold nights. Martin's money became valueless as soon as the war broke out. And Catherine and Leo's new house without doors was shaved into half by shells; it no longer needed doors.

There were many more people and stories in this city before the war, like Jennifer and her lesbian lover Cynthia, they never bored me. There was also James, the dyslexic bookstore owner, and Cindy the art curator who was admired and hated by all of the artists in this city. Although they were not without virtue and honor, it is the selfishness and vanity of humans that amused me most. I will tell their stories later.

As I am about to fall asleep, I hear meowing. A

kitten stares at me miserably in front of my box. It was probably born not long ago. Where is its mother? Does it have siblings? Alas. I have been a loner all my life, I never shared space with anyone else. It took me several seconds to consider, but then I decided I should walk away, leaving the cardboard box for the poor little thing. It's not hard to find another shelter, I am good and usually lucky in surviving. There must be somewhere else I can find in the dark alleyway. Tomorrow I will come here to check it and try to find some food for both of us.

Snowflakes begin to fall. I shudder a bit before walking forward in a manner as graceful as possible.

Originally published by *AUIS American University Iraq Sulaimani Literary Journal*

When The War Is Over, I Will Still Be Here

Do you hear the deafening choirs behind the walls? I do. I won't fall asleep until I hear them every night. They are the music replacing the memories of cries, screams, and wailing I had heard (or perhaps it was my own crying, screaming and wailing?) before being moved here. The music assures me that there are many people like me, at unknown corners all over the world, who never stopped relaying our dreams.

I am here because I wrote an anti-war poem and recited it at the foot of the Pushkin Monument in a small gathering. Later that night, four masked men in black uniforms broke into my apartment, beat me, carried me out, and threw me into their vehicle. I won't go into the details of what happened next; it was horrifying and disgusting.

Anyway, I am waiting for my sentence. But I can't recall if I had undergone any trial. The regime never bothered to hold a trial over the charge of "inciting hatred or enmity with the threat of violence".

How violent could a poem be? How much hatred could my poem incite? How could I threaten violence by being against the "special military operation" launched by the single decision-maker?

Over the past months (I lost count of how many), in sleepless nights, I began to recall stories I had heard in my youth. There were people put in jail by protesting against the junta, while others were exiled by standing against state terrorism. Some were confined by criticizing human rights violations by their rulers, and some were detained by making speeches that were considered endangered the national security. Some were missing because they published banned books, and some were abducted from their bookstores for displaying publications that offended the regime.

There is never a lack of reasons to erase a person.

I just did not imagine, by writing and reading a poem, I would become one of them.

I have asked myself one million times, would I do the same thing if time were reversed? There is no answer. I wasn't particularly brave or righteous, I simply voiced normal expectations and reasonable demands. I've begun my journey without any preparation, and I am not the first nor the only one. I am not an important person, nor am I completely insignificant.

From where I am, I can see a small piece of sky, although it is too small to rhyme. Once in a while, a bird flies by and my world vibrates for a second. I miss the moving sunbeams and changing landscape season by season, I miss the steam of very hot coffee in the morning, I miss the roaring cars beneath my windows. I miss the body heat when I embraced my fellow poets and protestors in falling snow. Where are they now? And do they know where I am now?

The war drags on, and I've started my journey without any expectations. I am not alone, nor will I be the last. I am not well-known, nor am I entirely forgotten by the world.

I miss making eye contact with the cat who often lounged in the bookstore I used to frequent. I miss the secret book readings my friends would organize in their tiny apartments. I miss my unpublished poems which might not be read by anymore.

Making us pay tremendous prices for our beliefs is like locking you all in the unwalled prison of fear and hopelessness. So I keep writing. When the war ends, the freedom fighters win back their dignity and identity, I will still be here. When the world celebrates the victory of democracy and the precious autonomy, my hair will turn gray, and my vision will fade away. But my ideas shall not be silenced, my idealism shall not age. I will still be read and remembered, for being heard is my delivery.

Can you hear the deafening sound of my poems being read outside of the walls? I do. What will last longer? Me, the dictator confining me, or my poetry?

I continue writing, because the more oppressive the regime is, the more people will become us. And the longer we are confined, the louder our works will become.

Do you hear the deafening choirs behind the walls?

Originally published by *Cease and Caesura*

Me, Nikolai, A Mercenary

It was odd to realize the immense power one could wield to bring destruction. Watching buildings crumble, entire communities burned down, and lives torn apart was both exciting and horrifying. I found myself strangely drawn to this dark and sadistic pleasure of causing damage. The thrill of violence seemed to captivate me, and the more chaos and devastation, the stronger the pull.

We had been roughly trained to use lethal weapons, and the focus of our training was not on self-protection or safeguarding our fellow soldiers. We were turned into killing machines, with our lives deemed dispensable. Relentlessness and fearlessness were ingrained in us. The battlefield became our playground, where we inflicted harm indiscriminately on people—civilians or combatants, men, women, or children, regardless of age or background.

I did not care to be killed, because our contract

said our family would be awarded a substantial amount of money if we died.

Nevertheless, one morning in the beginning of spring, after winning a bloody battle, we advanced several miles to occupy an evacuated farming village and swiped everything away, Viktor approached me and said in a low voice, "No need to be so brutal, you know. Take care of yourself."

"I don't care. I am earning a big prize for my mother."

"No more big prizes now. I was told that the families of dead soldiers no longer get money."

"Why is that?!"

"The bank of the big boss is drained."

"But is it in the contract?"

"You expect that your mom will hire a lawyer to sue the big boss if you die and she doesn't get the benefit payment?"

Suddenly, the thrill of the fighting I had imagined over the past months disappeared. I used to believe that I could keep fighting until I met my end—being shot or bombed. Then, when my mom received the big grant the big boss had promised, she would finally see my worth.

My mom always said I was born evil, a troublemaker. So, when she received the news of my sentence and imprisonment for robbery, she wasn't surprised. But she wasn't doing well herself, either. Mom drank too much, and when she was drunk, she'd go crazy. However, she'd also give me money generously in those moments. Since I was around eight, whenever I needed money, I'd steal alcohol from stores for her. Sometimes, I'd even sell it to friends.

But Mom's drinking problem got worse and worse, and a lot of time we fought after she drank. She was a strong woman, and I was a teenage boy, our fights often caused big damage. What did we fight for? I did not know. We just seemed to hate each other, and the smallest things could set us off. Looking back at how I spent my childhood and teenage years, I'd say she was the least qualified mother in the world.

And then I was arrested for robbery. I was trying to steal a bottle of liquor in a grocery store, but got busted by the store owner. He jumped on me and I struggled to break free from his grasp. That's how I went from being a thief to a robber and ended up being sentenced to a long time in jail.

So when someone showed up in the prison and offered me the opportunity to be set free, I took it immediately. I was born evil, and I did not care if it was moral to kill or to be killed. We became fighters after a short period of training in a children's vacation camp. The crash course did not make us good soldiers, but many of us had little to lose anyway, not to mention that we were paid much better than those drafted by the Department of National Defense.

But as the game rules were changed unilaterally, the fun was gone. Without the ultimate prize after my death, I would be nothing but wasted. I remembered that I once witnessed a cat torturing a bird it captured on a balcony. It was exciting to watch in the beginning, but after several minutes, when the bird was on the edge of death and gave up struggling, I was bored. I got up and left the balcony. And as I turned away, the cat stopped playing the dying bird. Surprised, I lingered a bit longer, and the cat resumed performing its game of death. I laughed and left. And as I got away from the balcony, the cat realized that it had failed to entertain its only audience. The show ended, and at that moment, the victim bird flew away with badly injured neck and wings. For unclear reasons, I gave the cat a glance of contempt, just like what my mom did to me so many times in my life.

If my mom didn't get a significant amount of money for my death, she would think I was a complete loser.

Each day I saw everyone of us, nothing but expendable killing machines who performed without an audience, I felt stupid. The freedom under blue sky is a false deal, and we never really earned it. I began to think about my survival, and how to get away from this mess.

Born evil, a convicted, me, Nikolai, a mercenary…

Run, Run, Run Away, Come Again Another Day

Once a proud and majestic feline, I now spend most of my days curling up in the corner of a bombed-out building, trying to avoid the deafening sounds of gunfire and explosions. I had witnessed many things in my life, but nothing quite like this.

For weeks, I had watched as people frantically packed up their belongings and fled the city, abandoning their homes and their possessions. It was difficult to see, even to a cat, that in many cases, they had to leave behind their elderly or ill family members because it was impossible to move them. At first people tried to leave in their vehicles, but soon realized that the traffic was too heavy, and the roads were blocked. They had to give up more things and start running on foot.

I considered leaving, too. But besides the frightening air raids, the panicked behavior of humans was also terrifying. Danger and uncertainty drove them crazy, they wailed, cursed, shouted, and began to turn against one another.

"See, that's the consequence of you voting for the Green Cross Party!"

"You think if the Blue Star Party won, we would be better off? Don't be naive. We will be enslaved under the expansion of imperialism!"

When the husband and wife were yelling to one another, a gray-haired man commented in a cold tone:

"Do you think the decision of invasion is based on your voting inclination? Do you think your arguments now can save the world? Smartasses."

So I decided to retreat to a temporary shelter, hoping to wait out the violence and destruction until it was safe to emerge again. Would it end soon? I had no idea, and neither did these desperate people.

As I watched the exodus from the roof of an evacuated house, I couldn't help but feel a sense of sadness and loss. Although these people were mediocre, selfish, and hypercritical, they were my people, my community. Now they were scattering in every direction, driven apart by the horrors of war.

During the first weeks of the evacuation, finding food was easy as most households had left behind plenty of provisions. Opening their refrigerators, pantries or cabinets, I could find meat, cheese, corn, eggs or bananas. However, the relentless bombardment eventually reduced the city to rubble and debris. With the power off, food stored in refrigerators decayed quickly. For days, I had been surviving on scraps and as I roamed the desolate streets in search of sustenance, my will was weakened by hunger.

I checked the home of the quarreling couple and found nothing but a half bottle of red wine. They had purchased the wine to celebrate their successful investment in Bitcoin. The fast surging price of the cryptocurrency before the war made them feel wealthy. Too bad that I couldn't take the wine, it was a very expensive French brew. They did not have any food at home, they always dined in fancy restaurants.

I walked into the destroyed theater. The gate was blown apart, and the walls were cracked. I moved toward the stage and carefully avoided the glass shards all over the floor. The seats were broken, with cushions and fabrics ripped. The ceiling fixtures swung under the badly damaged roof, they could fall at any moment. The floor of the stage sank, and the residual part of the burned curtains were hung on the distorted rail. All the stories that ever had been performed here had gone into oblivion, overwhelmed by the haunting stench of ruins. There was no food, no prey, not even a cockroach.

Two horse chestnuts by the theater stood amidst

the devastation, their trunks, branches and leaves were scorched during the rains of shells. It used to be a place filled with the chirping of birds, but now it was quiet. All the living beings had disappeared from here.

I adventured further to the home of Beatrice and Fedir. Fedir's ash was buried in their garden not long before the war. Fedir was 91 years old, so his passing wasn't a surprise to the community. But as a shrewd observer, or a sneaky peeper, I was sure Fedir's death was suicidal. Fedir had been aware that the invasion was imminent, but due to his age, it was impossible for him to travel hundreds of miles to reach the temporary shelters for refugees. He urged Beatrice, who was 55 years his junior, to leave without him. Despite his pleas, Beatrice refused to abandon Fedir and run off by herself. Having lived through World War II and the occupation of the same invader, Fedir feared that terrible things would happen to them if they stayed. He was particularly concerned about the safety of Beatrice, a young woman of great beauty, who would surely be a target of the military men known for their brutality and abuse. Fedir decided to stop drinking and eating, attempting to starve himself to death, so that Beatrice would be able to leave without worrying about him.

I'm not sure what the real cause of Fedir's death

was, but I have no doubt that to him, it was a release from the burden of his failing health. Fedir and Beatrice had been married for 13 years after meeting at a book club where they fell in love immediately. For the first several years of their marriage, they enjoyed each other's company, reading, traveling, and shopping together. However, as time passed, Fedir's health began to deteriorate rapidly, while Beatrice was in her prime. She adapted to Fedir's pace and waited on him hand and foot. Despite her devotion, Fedir felt that, almost throughout their marriage, Beatrice was doing nothing but waiting, waiting—for him. She took him to doctors, to get sunlight on good days, or to funerals of old friends. She took care of him when he used the restroom, and she bathed him tenderly and ritually every night. In fact, Fedir felt not only like a prisoner to his own declining body but Beatrice's sacrifice, and although she never complained, Fedir was convinced that Beatrice was trapped in her responsibility to care for him, as well as the credit their community gave her. Being virtuous could be a confinement. Eventually, the threat of war prompted Fedir to make a drastic decision.

But it was my assumption. Who am I to be credible in making such a conclusion?

I crept through the ruins until I came to a collapsed building of a supermarket. Inside, amidst the wreckage, I discovered a stash of canned meat and fish. There must be adored cats living around this neighborhood. I began clawing and scratching at the tins until they finally gave way and devoured the contents of each can with ravenous hunger. After finishing my first full meal in a long time, I licked my paws and whiskers to restore my elegance.

Between air-raids, the streets of the city were quiet, although the distant rumble of tanks was heard occasionally. It was a drill, our army was trained to operate the tanks, among other military vehicles, sent to us from far away by our allies. As I arrived downtown, I noticed the door of the Irish pub was hanging off its hinges. Upon entering, I saw the tables and chairs were overturned, and smashed bottles and glasses were scattered around. It was evident that the damage was done by looting, not by bombing.

An episode in the pub I had witnessed a couple of years ago resurfaced in my mind. It was a typical Saturday night, the cozy establishment was buzzing with energy as the evening crowd settled in, amidst their low chatter and clinking of glasses in the dimly lit space, a light sweet scent of e-cigarettes filled the air. I recalled seeing Monica, a theater actress, approach a lone traveler. Her sky blue dress provided a stark contrast to the red wine she held in hand, and the few steps she took towards him convinced me that she could outdo me on the catwalk.

A DJ arrived to entertain the customers, and the *My Wild Irish Rose* he first played turned on the entire place instantly. Monica and the man got on their feet and swayed to the center of the pub, they danced in the loving song. Monica's blue dress swirled around her knees, and her smile radiated. They moved fluidly, and exchanged words while their faces were close to each other's. I rested in a seat at their table and noticed Monica's facial muscles began to show a little bit of rigidity. I was curious, and I watched them closely. When the music was about to end, I read Monica's lips, "Fuck off. You don't belong here," while struggling to maintain a fake smile.

I did not remember what happened afterward, but looking back, I realized that their quarrel was not that of ex-lovers, but rather political. Their dance was a negotiation which broke up. Political manipulation between hostile entities had been ongoing long before the outbreak of war, but the public ignored it.

I left the pub and walked into the House of God. The altar lay in ruins, the nave charred by a fierce blaze, and the fragments of the fallen cupola now scattered on the floor. As I surveyed the devastation, my eyes fell upon burned copies of Bibles and amputated icons of saints among the debris. The gallery above appeared to be in imminent danger of collapsing. The priest and his staff had stayed in the beginning of the invasion, hoping to provide safety and comfort for people who did not flee and sought shelter. They were wrong to assume that the holy place wouldn't be razed. The destruction of the aggressors was indiscriminate.

Where is Monica now? Where is Beatrice? I looked up at the sky, not knowing when the shells would fall from heaven next time.

"You don't belong here." I heard it again.

How much should we recede to find our peace?

Originally published by *Story Sanctum*

The Enduring Testament of Human Cruelty

I am a street cat. Before the war I was over 12 pounds, and I've lost weight and now weigh under 10 pounds since the war erupted. I know this because I witnessed a man triggering a landmine and being killed at a spot I'd walked by. It was a mess. No appropriate funeral could be held for him because no one dared to dig in this area, not even walking around. An anti-personnel landmine could be triggered by a human child who is bigger than a starving cat, not to mention any adult.

I suppose my constant hunger has saved my life. It's no wonder even after the army withdrew, no villagers came back to their homes. The landmines prevented their return.

In the twilight, I wandered through the streets, hoping to find some food left by the troops once stationed here. With great caution, I treaded softly across the broken terrain, relying on my senses to guide me through the treacherous paths.

The place was completely devoid of life. If there was food, it must have gone bad by now. In despair, I decided to find a shed and take a nap. I was so tired.

By the time I woke up, it was the dawn of another day. I must be really exhausted last night, it was a long sleep. In the morning breeze, I discovered some berries amidst the weed by the shed and I immediately ate them all. They were sour but juicy, and they restored my energy to a certain degree.

If there were berries, there might be some other fruits around. I looked up the trees, attempting to identify some fruit trees among the damaged ones caused by bombings.

My whiskers twitched when I heard something. Who else could be here? I certainly did not want to encounter another victim of landmines. Fortunately, it was a bird, a bullfinch. Usually I would play with birds, chasing them, capturing them and torturing them for fun. But Today I wasn't in that mood, and I knew, as it was easy to observe an orange bird, following it could lead me to fruit trees or flowers with honey.

The entire place is now my territory, belonging to no one but myself. I find solace in being away from any human presence, whether they be perpetrators or victims. It is a gratifying feeling to have a space that is exclusively mine, and it is equally rewarding to have decent companions, particularly those who dwell in the sky rather than on land and possess the ability to find sustenance.

I imagine this place remaining uninhabited for the next few decades, as landmines can remain active for up to fifty years, surpassing the lifespan of many structures. Even after the war has ended and soldiers have demobilized, even after the people who once called this place home may have perished, yet the haunting danger of landmines lingers. Despite being buried underground, the desolation they have caused will be an enduring testament to human cruelty.

Originally published by *Where Meadows Reside*

A Lighthouse in Memory

Olena woke up to an eerie silence. For months, the relentless noise of bombardment and shelling had never ceased; people of the port town had endured deafening air raids, both near and far, around the clock. Thus the sudden, unexpected silence implied that the lighthouse, along with other port facilities, had finally been destroyed, as the aggressors had intended since the outbreak of the war.

Olena took the job as the lighthouse keeper from her father Mikhail, who inherited this position from his father Ivan. Respectively they accomplished the missions of restoration from the ravages of military conflicts during the great war and the modernization of the antiquated facilities.

When Olena's mother left them, Mikhail had to take his baby girl to his work. Olena grew up with the sound of the waves and the light of the beacon as her constant companions. She learned to navigate the intricacies of the lighthouse's machinery from her father's various engineering tasks.

Through one hundred and fifty years of oceanic swell and ebb, the lighthouse bears witness to the port's spasmodic changes of prosperity and decline, succumbing to the whimsy of global political tides. As the war broke out, the port became a strategic target. Missiles and shells rain down, turning the once bustling docks into twisted metal and rubble.

Now the lighthouse was gone, swiped off from the earth, and all ships would avoid coming to the besieged port. Throughout her lifetime, Olena's perspective of the world has been 26-meter high; she felt disoriented on the ground with views blocked by buildings. Olena sent a notice to mariners, a warning about the damage to the port radio station and the port authority. Despite the chaos, Olena was told a medical boat was scheduled to arrive in a couple of hours. She packed things up and began to walk northwestward. There were 4 KM ahead of her before nightfall.

***

The night was thickening with smoke and the acrid scent of burning debris. The port was shrouded in darkness as the lighthouse lay in ruins.

The medical boat Hope No.3 navigated the

treacherous waters, its crew desperate to reach the harbor. Captain Thompson's eyes strained from the smoke and darkness, scanning the horizon for any sign of guidance.

Suddenly, a flicker of light caught his eye. On a hill, a fire blazed, its flames dancing against the night sky. Captain Thompson steered the boat towards the fire, the crew working quietly to navigate the perilous waters. One wrong turn, they'd be dashed against the unforgiving shore.

As they drew closer, the fire's glow and its reflection on water illuminated the path. The boat edged into the harbor, guided by the makeshift beacon.

***

As the boat safely harbored and the flames gradually died down, Olena set up a tent to rest. From her pack, she took out a blueprint of the lighthouse and studied it once more. She had to commit every detail to memory.

***

My Dear fellow townspeople:

I write to you from a place that once stood tall,

a beacon of hope and guidance for those lost at sea. My name is Olena, and for many years, I was the keeper of this lighthouse. I took the job from my father, and my father took the job from his father. To me, the lighthouse was more than just a structure of stone and light; it was the legacy of my family, as well as a symbol of resilience, a guardian of the coast, and a silent witness to the tides of time. But the war left nothing but ruins in its wake.

I had remembered every detail of the lighthouse's structure and prayed everyday that it could be reconstructed, but as I stood among the remnants of what was once my home and my duty, I realized rebuilding the lighthouse would erase the scars of the past, and the ruins themselves hold a far greater significance.

The lighthouse, in its broken state, is a powerful reminder of the fragility of peace and democracy. It stands as a testament to the immense cost of conflict and the lives irrevocably changed by it.

Let these remnants serve as the evidence to all who suffered and sacrificed. Let the site be a place where future generations can come to reflect on the cruelty the innocent people had endured.

The light of the lighthouse may no longer shine, but its memory can still guide us—not to the safe harbor, but to a world where we strive for peace and understanding of our autonomy. No other forms of monument could be more authentic than the relics caused by war, more stunning than the destruction of humanity.

When visiting the site, let all who come stumble upon the ruins and be reminded of the dark times in our history.

Sincerely Yours,
Olena
Former Keeper of the Lighthouse

***

The rain fell in a steady drizzle as Daniel Thompson stood on the edge of the crumbling pier, his coat collar turned up against the chill. Before him lay the skeletal remains of the lighthouse, its once-proud structure now a jagged silhouette against the gray sky. His father, Captain Thompson, had spoken of this place often—how during the war, the lighthouse had been destroyed by shelling, leaving the port in darkness. But the medical boat had still come, guided by fires set on the nearby hill, to bring assistance to those who couldn't flee.

Daniel stepped closer, his boots sinking into the muddy ground. The air smelled of salt and decay, the harbor quiet except for the soft lapping of waves against the rocks. He imagined his father standing here many years ago, the medical boat cutting through the black water, its crew ready to tend to the wounded and the sick. The elderly, the children, the ones who couldn't leave—they had waited here, their faces gaunt with fear and hope.

Earlier Daniel had climbed the uneven path to the hill where the fires had burned. The grass was slick with rain, the scene of wind carrying the faint tang of smoke surfaced, though no fire had burned here in years. About half way up the peak, he paused to look down at the ruined lighthouse and the harbor beyond. He could almost see the flicker of flames, hear the shouts of the crew as they unloaded supplies, his father's voice steady and calm amid the chaos.

Daniel knelt, brushing his fingers over the stones, imaging the charred marks caused by the fires set up for the medical boat. The rain grew heavier, soaking through Daniel's coat, but he stayed a moment longer. He thought of the lives saved and the hands his father had held. The place, broken and forgotten, had once been a beacon of survival.

On the memorial plaque next to the commemorative lighthouse relics, Daniel scanned the QR code, which led him to images of the lighthouse, including views overlooking the port, the ocean, and the sky. There were also diagrams of the lighthouse's architecture and the machines that kept the light beams turning. As an architect, Daniel especially appreciated the drawings. He downloaded and saved them on his smartphone.

As he turned to leave, Daniel whispered a quiet thanks—to the lighthouse, to the hill, and to the unknown guardians who had kept the fires burning. He put his smartphone in his pocket; now, he had the lighthouse saved in his memory.

Afterword—
Bookstores in Taiwan

I told the bookstores in Taiwan selling my books that I'd include them in my acknowledgement. However, considering the challenges faced by bookstores in Hong Kong and the surprising growth of the publishing industry and bookstores in Ukraine, I decided to write something about how essential bookstores are to us.

Bookstores often reflect the cultural vibrancy of a city and how its people identify with their culture and communities. They stimulate a city's intellectual and social dynamism, becoming landmarks in their own right, drawing readers and fostering a sense of place. Bookstores provide a platform for voices from different backgrounds and perspectives, promoting a rich tapestry of cultural expressions.

Freedom of speech is perhaps the most significant contribution of bookstores. They provide access to a wide array of ideas and perspectives, supporting the free exchange of information and the right to read and think independently. By stocking books that challenge the status quo and present diverse viewpoints, bookstores uphold the principles of intellectual freedom and resist censorship. This role is vital in maintaining a healthy, democratic society where individuals are encouraged to explore and express their ideas freely.

In Taiwan, independent bookstores have carved out a special niche, playing critical roles in preserving and promoting local culture. These bookstores often focus on niche markets, offering books that may not be found in larger chains, including works by local authors and publications on regional history and culture. They not only provide unique literary offerings but also serve as venues for cultural exchange and community engagement.

Although almost all bookstores face market challenges, their persistence sustains the hungry minds of diverse readers. Such a dream is no longer realized in places like Hong Kong, where freedom of speech has been deprived.

Lastly, special thanks to Bookman Bookstore, Kuo's Astral Bookshop, Garden City Book Shop, and DH Cafe. They showcase my books, which are otherwise difficult to sell, allowing my ideas to reach readers from all over the world.

About the Author

C. J. Anderson-Wu(吳介禎)is a Taiwanese writer and translator known for her compelling works that delve into Taiwan's military dictatorship era, specifically the White Terror period (1949-1987). She has published two notable collections: *Impossible to Swallow* (2017) and *The Surveillance* (2021).

Her works have been shortlisted for several international literary awards, including the Art of Unity Creative Award by the International Human Rights Art Festival, and Fly Island Poetry Manuscript Contest. She has also won the Strands Lit International Flash Fiction Competition, the Invisible City Blurred Genre Literature Competition, and the Wordweavers Literature Contest.

C. J. Anderson-Wu's writing is characterized by its deep exploration of historical and political themes, as well as its emotional intensity. Her contributions to literature have been recognized and celebrated globally, making her a significant voice in contemporary Taiwanese literature.

Author	C. J. Anderson-Wu
Sponsor & Publisher	Kanda Yasuko Family Memorial Foundation
Editors	Ginny Jaramillo, Steven M. Anderson
Art Editor	Ya-Yun Chung
ISBN	978-626-01-3942-1
Date	May 2025
Cover Price	350 NTD, 12 USD

Special Thanks to Cover Artist Ludou Lin
Artificial Landscape II—Forest of the Dead, 2011

www.ingramcontent.com/pod-product-compliance
Lightning Source LLC
LaVergne TN
LVHW011937070526
838202LV00054B/4692